Also by Maureen Gilmer

*Growing Vegetables in Drought,
Desert & Dry Times*

The Small Budget Gardener

Palm Springs–Style Gardening

California Wildfire Landscaping

Water Works

Gaining Ground

The Colorful Dry Garden

Over 100 Flowers and Vibrant Plants
for Drought, Desert & Dry Times

Maureen Gilmer

SASQUATCH BOOKS
SEATTLE

Dedicated with gratitude to Jeanne Fredericks, my friend, agent, and lifelong literary partner

Printed in China
Published by Sasquatch Books

22 21 20 19 18   9 8 7 6 5 4 3 2 1

Editor: Hannah Elnan | **Production editor:** Bridget Sweet
Design: Bryce de Flamand | **Copyeditor:** Kristin Vorce Duran

Cover Photographs: © Maureen Gilmer (front cover top two photographs and back cover photographs), © Saxon Holt (front cover bottom two photographs), © Creative Market.com | Jim Harter – flower illustration (back cover)

Interior Photographs: © Creative Market.com | Jim Harter – plant and flower illustrations (pgs i, iii, iv, v, x, xi, 24, 25, 207, 214), © iStock.com | csfotoimages – Blue Californian Lilac flowers (pg 57), © IanRedding | Shutterstock.com – Wild thyme (Thymus serpyllum) (pg 64), © Lookatmy | Dreamstime.com– Vinca major leaves and flowers (pg 65), © iStock.com | kathyclark777 – Alabama Wildflower Coreopsis tinctoria (pg 105), © iStock.com | karimitsu – Portulaca oleracea (pg 112), © Huy Thoai | Dreamstime.com – Portulaca grandiflora (pg 112), © HGalina | Shutterstock.com – Cineraria Maritime (Senecio cineraria) (pg 114), © attilavalentina | Shutterstock.com – Harlequin flowers (Sparaxis tricolor) (pg 119), © iStock.com | bluehill75 – African Iris (pg 130), © iStock.com | aimintang – Torch Lily (pg 134), © aniana | Shutterstock.com – Lavender, Lavandula angustifolia, Lavandula officinalis (pg 135), © Ivan Marc | Shutterstock.com – Lavender field, Lavandula dentata (pg 136), © iStock.com | LianeM – Jerusalem sage, Phlomis russeliana (pg 141), © iStock.com | QUAYSIDE – Santolina chamaecyparissus (pg 146), © Sagegardenherbs | Dreamstime.com – Lamb`s Ears Stachys byzantina (pg 147), © Chris Moncrieff | Dreamstime.com – Zauschneria

Califomnica (pg 148), © iStock.com | Rostislavv – Persian silk tree (Albizia julibrissin) flowers (pg 179 both photos), © iStock.com | AlessandraRC – Arbutus unedo (strawberry tree) flowers (pg 180), © iStock.com | ajcastillo – El Madroño (pg 180), © iStock.com | Yuldoshov – Chitalpa tashkentensis (pg 183), © Wiert Nieuman | Shutterstock.com – x Chitalpa tashkentensis (= Chilopsis linearis x Catalpa bignonioides) (pg 183), © Dmitry Strizhakov | Shutterstock.com – Silk floss tree flowers (Ceiba speciosa) (pg 184), © iStock.com | valentinacalatrava – Ceiba speciosa (silk floss tree) (pg 185), © iStock.com | victorn – Ceiba speciosa pink flowers (pg 185), © iStock.com | igaguri_1 – Flowers of the crape myrtle (pg 187), © iStock.com | vsanderson – Crepe Myrtle Tree Blossoms (pg 187), © iStock.com | BasieB – Robinia pseudoacacia – Scheinakazie (pg 189), © iStock.com | Orchidpoet – Pink-Flowered Locust Tree (pg 189), © iStock.com | BasieB – Vitex agnus-castus, Mönchspfeffer (pg 190 both photos), © iStock.com | ClaraNila – Prunus laurocerasus with white flowers (pg 196), © iStock.com | mtreasure – Bay tree specimen-plant (laurus nobilis) (pg 196), © iStock.com | killerbayer – Olive blossom (pg 197), © iStock.com | joloei – Dragon fruit (pg 203)

Photographs on pages 2, 12, 26, 52, 74, 98, 122, 152, 174, 192 by Saxon Holt
Map illustrations by Hannah Small
All other photographs by Maureen Gilmer

Library of Congress Cataloging-in-Publication Data is available.

ISBN: 978-1-63217-063-7

Sasquatch Books
1904 Third Avenue, Suite 710 | Seattle, WA 98101
(206) 467-4300 | www.sasquatchbooks.com
custserv@sasquatchbooks.com

Contents

Introduction

Drought has always been a part of the American West, with historic reports of cyclical dry spells dating back to the Spanish period. As demand for water rises as our cities and their suburbs grow, the current supply won't be enough under normal rainfall. Add drought to such stressed infrastructure and it's clear the impact will be immediate and significant. And unless you can come to terms with the water demands of your current garden, it will become a perpetual unsightly brownout as dry continues to become the new normal.

It's time to reconsider some drought-loving plants you may already know and discover some new ones that make great substitutes for the moisture lovers you're currently harboring. Don't worry, there are many beautiful flowering options for bright color in the often all-too-monochromatic xeriscape or desert garden!

As a California horticulturist, I share a deep interest in the ornamental garden and its evolution. I am a lover of vintage architecture and roses and so many plants that have lost favor because of their water-loving characteristics. The problem today is that designers have sacrificed flowers for succulents and grasses. Blossoms are seen more as pollinator havens than providers of striking beauty. We need color in drought too! Those succulents and grasses need flowers to add interesting hues, particularly in the seasons when they are drab or dormant.

I've been making plant lists for over 30 years. My projects from the 1970s drought and my residential landscapes in the Sonoran and Mojave Deserts have allowed me to develop the optimal palette for droughty locations everywhere. These lists streamline my plant selection process because I know they are proven over time. This book evolved out of all my lists for color in desert and other arid climates that make the perfect palette for those working to overcome drought with a beautiful, floriferous drier garden. This book lends a designer's understanding of contemporary and traditional West Coast styles for residential landscaping, and it provides the horticulturist's view on cultivation problems and a passion for flowers. And it will give every gardener the same knowledge I use when seeking the right plant for the right space.

This book is organized into two parts. Part I will take you through the process of transitioning to a drier garden. Because everyone's landscape is unique, you can tailor the way you change your garden to suit your needs, budget, and time frame. Whether you redo your garden all at once or just plan a long incremental series of smaller changes, these basics will help you make the best choices from the very start. More garden remodeling efforts fail because of gardeners misunderstanding these basics than any other cause.

Part II makes up our plant compendium of carefully selected species that will add flowers and color to your garden without using much water. They are organized by their role in the garden, from permanent structure (shrubs) to the canopy (trees) to perennials that can create an arid border every bit as beautiful as an English garden. One chapter focuses solely on issues of the ground plane, which are serious when you take out a lawn and must relandscape. Organizing the plants by their design function makes it more intuitive to find the plants you need easily rather than having to sift through a more scientific horticultural approach.

The exception is our primary use of botanical names because many succulents and natives lack well-known common names (or have a dozen of them). You'll need this nomenclature to ensure you get the right plant, particularly when it comes to new introductions or obscure species.

Above all, your home is the most important investment you will ever make. Allowing a landscape to wither with climate change will cost you money every single day. Moreover, when it comes time to sell, a sustainable landscape of beautiful flowering plants on quality drip irrigation will be the irresistible element that closes the deal.

Resorting to a dull, monochromatic modern look is not necessary when coping with drought. I hope this book helps you bring your garden alive with flowers and color, with birds and butterflies, so that it changes with the seasons and yet asks for few resources. Let orchid trees bloom overhead, thyme flower beneath your feet, bougainvillea drape the walls, and fabulous succulents ring around the pool. Plant with impunity from this book and you may not even notice if drought becomes the new normal.

PART I
Going Dry

Guidelines for Transition to an Arid Palette

President Bill Clinton has stated that "the price of doing the same old thing is far higher than the price of change." Nowadays, the cost of doing the same old thing in your garden is manifest in receiving sky-high water bills, facing financial penalties for failing to conserve, or raising the ire of your drought-compliant neighbors. It's a lot less expensive in the long run to remake your garden than struggling to keeping thirsty plants alive until the drought ends. The truth is, if climate change proves permanent, the drought may become our new normal. Failing to make a change now will cost you money and leave your home landscape looking dead and dry forever. In the long run you'll end up making the same change anyway if rains fail to return as they should. Thus changing our planting designs now begins the long process required for long-lived plants to reach their mature beauty.

Remaking your garden with drought-resistant plants is a design project. The result may be similar to how your old landscape looked by simply using visually matching drought-resistant plants the same way thirsty ones functioned within the design before. Or yours may be a whole garden redesign, which allows a fresh new look and feel by changing out all the plants. This is also the perfect time to replace your lawn or solid paving with gravel, unit pavers, or flagstones that allow rain to percolate down to recharge the water table.

When to Do It

Remaking a garden can happen during the growing season, but it's best done in the western states in the fall. This gives the new plants all winter and spring with uniform soil moisture to adapt before the summer heat and low humidity strikes. While you can replant a garden in spring where summers are milder along the coast and in the high country, these plants face a daunting summer almost immediately.

Degrees of Change

Each person's garden is unique, so the way you approach it will be based on your site, climate, and lifestyle. The extent of this adaption to greater drought resistance and the way you approach it will be unique too. Here are the options:

Individual plant replacement. This one-for-one exchange is the easiest way to bring great-looking new plants in to replace old ones struggling on low water supply. Be aware that existing irrigation may not suit the new plant's lower demands without adjusting watering frequency, duration, and delivery methods.

....

Replace a section. This approach allows you to replace most or all plants in a high-profile location with a more design-oriented palette of drought-resistant species. When done with respect for existing sprinkler valve zones, you can switch the entire planting zone to a drip system more easily using the same original valve.

....

Redo beds and borders. Whether it's the front-yard foundation planting or your flower bed visible from the kitchen, beds and borders are where former annual and perennial flower gardens demanded nearly as much water supply as a lawn. Flower gardeners will find these new plants a great way to save water by replanting with vivid bloomers from dry climates. Here existing spray heads may be replaced with low-flow heads, or they may be adapted to low-pressure micro-spray irrigation.

....

Replace the whole garden. Often it costs nearly the same to relandscape as it does to replace plants in fits and starts. This is the xeriscape designer's dream, to create a whole new look and provide optimal irrigation with the latest moisture-sensing technology.

....

The Process

Creating and changing a landscape is done through a process, a series of universal steps that tell you or a designer what comes next. It ensures you consider what's important both aesthetically and on a more practical level so everything works well together in the end. If you approach it without process, the result is often disjointed.

Step 1 **Establish the scope of your project.** Begin your process by considering the scale of your project, which designers call "limit of work." Avoid thinking outside this limit to keep things simple and focused. If you are uncomfortable with a bigger approach, repeat this process for each area or plant when you're ready to move on.

Step 2 **Determine your budget.** This factor tells you how much replanting you can do with funds available. If you don't remove the older plants yourself, make sure you allow for costs of demolition that should include hauling those dead or dying old plants to the dump or chipper. This will have to cover irrigation changes too, particularly on larger projects. The biggest cost is new plants you intend to buy. In general, buying most plants in 1-gallon ($5 to $7 each) or 5-gallon containers ($15 to $20 each) is the most affordable way to make the change. When you go up to larger 15-gallon specimens, the price can rise from $20 to $150 for an older plant of the exact same species.

Step 3 **Gather supplies for design.** Round up everything you'll need to draw a plan so the process goes smoothly. Just sketching your yard helps with brainstorming, but what you really need to create great changes and stay on budget is a basic to-scale drawing of the yard. The scale should be ¼ inch = 1 foot for small areas or city spaces. A suburban home may need to go to ⅛ inch = 1 foot to fit on your sheet. Most can be drawn on an 11-by-17-inch page or an 18-by-22-inch page. An architect's scale for drafting is sold in every school supply section at office supply chain stores for under $10. You can also try gridded paper or vellum. Use a soft lead pencil and buy a *big* eraser, which works better on vellum than regular paper.

Step 4 **Measure your site and locate control plants, which are those to remain.** The easy way to measure is with a 30-foot tape, a piece of paper, and a pencil. Begin by sketching the yard on the paper starting with the perimeter around the edges, then work your way in until all the planting areas are shown. Then go back and measure the length of each perimeter, including the walls of your house that border the garden, and note everything you see that influences the area of your project. Write in the length of each line next to them in feet and inches, such as 3'4". Draw solid circles for each plant that is to remain.

Step 5 Draw your plan to scale. By drawing to scale, you can draw your plants in at the full size they will grow to be. Measure the space with your architect's scale and then find a plant that is sized perfectly for that application. One of the biggest causes of unnecessary maintenance is overly large woody plants that exceed their allowable space. When drawing in at scale you can be sure that the little plant will grow up to fit perfectly in the space provided without shearing, pruning, or hacking it down to size every year after.

Step 6 Identify plants to be replaced. When creating a larger project, this aspect of the plan will be vital to showing others what plants should be removed and hauled away. It also lets you see it all in plan view (the top-down bird's-eye view) to decide if maybe you want other changes to better suit the newer plants. If a plant that's doing well doesn't work with what you want for the future, feel free to take it out too. This may allow you to make a better composition with the replacement and its companions.

Step 7 Evaluate locations of removed plants for criteria. Every planting area that you identify on the plan will experience its own conditions depending on various factors, such as what shade-giving elements influence that space. Under trees that are staying, for example, plants that are dying from drought will need replacements that want the same shady conditions. Evaluate each area and then make sure plants you choose from this book share the same sun requirements (full sun, part sun, or shade). They may also prefer a hot afternoon exposure or a milder morning sun-drenched site. See the site assessment section that follows for more details on this.

Step 8 Choose plants that fit. This is the art of choosing the right plant, something designers grapple with all the time. You must think in three dimensions of height, width, and length to get this right. Each plant in this book has a designated diameter and height at near maturity so you can draw a circle that size on the plan to ensure it fits. Make sure the plant is tall enough to screen a neighbor or short enough to avoid blocking the window. When all the plants are chosen and placed on your plan in lieu of those removed, make your plant list and count how many of each you will need. This turns your plan into an accurate cost estimating tool at the nursery, for demolition, and for any other larger changes you have in mind.

Site Assessment

As you work through the process of creating a step-by-step plan, here are some details that will help you better understand your immediate conditions and what they mean.

EXPOSURE

This is how the sun affects the particular spot you're working on. Consider the desired exposure of your new drought-resistant replacement plants. These four conditions are used to refer to sides of a house and the general exposure in planting areas on each one:

> **Southern:** This is optimal for sun exposure all day long without direct access to extreme afternoon heat.
>
> ....
>
> **Eastern:** Plants here receive morning sun with protection in the afternoon for a soft and gentle growing ground.
>
> ....
>
> **Western:** This is the hot zone where high heat and intense sun literally bake all but the most resilient natives or desert plants that demand high summer temperatures.
>
> ....
>
> **Northern:** Very few plants will thrive in this location, which is almost always in the shade.
>
> ....

SHADY INFLUENCES

Shadows are the transients of the garden cast by both on-site and off-site influences. For example, a large shadow in your yard may be cast by your tree or one next door. Whether that tree is evergreen or deciduous is vital to exposures in spring and fall. Shade cast by taller multistory buildings is permanent. The angle and extent of shade cast by trees can be changed by thinning the canopy to make it more transparent so shadows are lightened to make shade brighter.

EARTH BENEATH YOUR FEET

Most backyard soils are quite suitable but certain xeriscape species originate in specific soil conditions that affect fertility and drainage. Desert plants, cacti, succulents, and alpine species all desire a similar fast-draining, lean, granular soil. Mediterraneans often originate in conditions like those of inland valleys. California natives thrive in foothill locations where topography speeds runoff.

> **Coasts:** Salt air can influence sandy soils in beach communities all along the Pacific Coast where alkalinity builds up to very high pH. Just inland from the beaches, soils can transition to bluffs of very heavy clay with normal pH but serious drainage issues unless the ground is sloping.

> **Inland valleys:** Our best agricultural soils are on the valley bottomlands where conditions are clay and silt, with very high fertility. Plants that love lean ground will have problems, but just about everything else thrives there.

> **Foothills:** These transitional zones between the valleys and mountains are rarely flat sites and almost always sloping, which is helpful for drainage. Very dense clay subsoils can hide drainage problems on more level ground. Typically heavy, rocky clays, sometimes with acidic low pH, are difficult to dig but often quite fertile. Many popular natives originate in these plant communities.

Mountains: The combination of extreme winter cold and rocky infertile ground offers great opportunities for rock gardens using local natives that will likely naturalize on slopes and rocky fields.

....

High desert: These very dry regions can experience hardpan drainage issues in low-lying areas while super-porous alluvial ground created by epic erosion is rocky and infertile. Extremely low rainfall and cold winters make this a real challenge to traditional plants, but those from similar habitats thrive there with scant irrigation.

....

Low desert: Most of these zones are plagued with very fine sand, dune sand, and gravelly ground that can vary in fertility. Water moves straight through, so keeping roots adequately moist requires very carefully designed irrigation so plants survive soaring summers that can reach 120 degrees F in July and August.

....

EXISTING PLANTS

Every landscape plant adds value to the visual beauty of your home landscape. Some plants do more by providing shade and protection for places around your home. Trees that offer shade in summer and bare branches in winter directly affect energy consumption. These hardworking plants are so important they are worth watering, even if it means shorting other less essential ones.

IDENTIFY THOSE TO REMAIN

It takes a long time, often decades, for some landscape plants to reach maturity. This makes each and every one valuable because the cost of replacing them with specimens is prohibitive for most. If that tree or shrub or vine is vital to how your property functions, it may influence so many other plants that the result is shocking. For example, if your tree is struggling, removal can destroy all associated landscaping because the plants around it will lose the protection and fry in the sun.

These older, slower-growing, long-lived species number among the most irreplaceable because they can take a decade to reach full size. Experts have determined a mature shade tree can increase home value by as much as $10,000 each. This points to the most important aspect of this whole process: deciding what plants must remain for their intrinsic value, their contribution to conditions in the yard, and their sheer irreplaceability (think of mature plants with a magnitude that takes a human lifetime to achieve).

Here's what to look for:

- Healthy shade trees that are impossible to replace because transplanting mature specimens can take far more water to help them become established. Don't rely on big boxed landscape trees as replacement because you won't have the water to give them either.

- Mature woody vines trained to shade arbors, which are essential to the quality of the space underneath. These are usually outdoor living spaces, patios, and porches that would be uncomfortable without them. If these vines are lost the time required to regain such shade may be at least a decade of growth.

- Large shrubs that may be classified as small trees. These special forms of large shrubs, such as toyon and Indian hawthorn, have been used as street trees in high-density Southern California neighborhoods. Though shrubs, consider these irreplaceable trees too.

- Large shrubs that offer screening or wind breaks. This is about comfort and privacy, and nothing works like a screen hedge to keep your spa area suitable for skinny-dipping. Nurture these linear plantings that make outdoor living possible in areas of perpetual breezes or wind because it takes a lot of plants to replace a hedge, which is very expensive.

- Large deciduous flowering shrubs. These are the old workhorses of gardens in the West such as forsythia, flowering quince, and naturalized lilacs. Most can survive drought with a few hand waterings to withstand periodic dry spells. These shrubs are such welcome early spring color that for many homes in historic neighborhoods they are part of the architectural statement.

- Exceptionally slow-growing long-lived plants. Gardeners who have nurtured their favorite plants for years will not want to start over with slow growers. These can be older plants established in century-old homes or occasional exotics such as sago palm that haven't changed in 300 million years and will likely survive drought. Know what plant you're looking at and read about its demands because it may prove far more resilient than you think.

○ All existing drought-resistant species. You may not recognize your existing drought-resistant species, so make sure to identify every plant you can before you make changes. Few people truly know what's growing out there, so it's a good idea to solicit the aid of a plant expert to help you identify those plants that are there and established. They'll be able to help you know what's worthy of saving among the drought plants and what traditionals are worth saving on a newly purchased home. Often full-service garden centers have folks you can hire for an hour or two to help you identify your landscape and evaluate the health and longevity of what should remain.

Once you've gone through the process and considered all the criteria in this chapter, you will know your home landscape far better than you ever imagined. Above all, understand that plant choice isn't just putting pretty flowering plants in your yard to save water. It involves learning what you have, naming your plants, and knowing their general requirements. Each, like children, will have its own character, personality, and degree of vigor. And for those who take the plunge and create a plan for your garden, the plants in Part II will give you all the color you're dreaming of with half the water, and the vision to put it all together.

Protect Trees at All Times

Whenever gardens are relandscaped, there's always concern for the health of the plants to remain. Trenching for new irrigation, removing lawns with trees in them, increasing foot and vehicle traffic, disturbing surface soil, and doing other activities can stress root systems and even change them. Above all, respect the dripline of each tree and woody plant to remain. The dripline is the outer edge of the canopy projected down to the ground. Consider every square foot of soil within this dripline priceless because it's where tree roots congregate. Use brightly colored stakes and string or plastic net fence to rope off these very sensitive areas so the roots and the soil in the root zone are not disturbed in the process. Some trees such as native oaks have highly sensitive roots that die when soil around them is compacted by foot traffic. Others will send up suckers where roots are nicked or broken. Those with fine surface feeder roots can reduce moisture uptake potential if the roots are severed.

Your Microclimate: Regional Differences and Climatic Limitations

No matter where you live, it's essential to get a handle on the local climate, including its opportunities and limitations. It is important to know what plants grow locally based on the USDA Plant Hardiness Zone Map. Because many drought-resistant plants are not particularly cold hardy, this is important if you live in cooler climes or higher elevations. Use it to match western natives and exotics to your local zone. Virtually all plants need irrigation in the West because even the hardy natives are dying out in the wild for lack of rainfall.

Every garden design student is taught the age-old mantra: select the right plant for the right place. This may seem overly simple but, in fact, it's quite complex. It's what makes selecting a plant far more challenging than choosing decorative elements indoors. If unhappy because it's too hot, too cold, too wet, or too dry, a plant will languish and eventually die. Worse yet, when the designer fails to make the right selection in terms of size, the result is the perpetual hacking back of a too-large plant or the disappointment and crimes against horticulture that eventually result from downsizing with power tools. But when you have the right plant for the space, the results aren't just that the plant lives, but it looks its best every day and remains relatively maintenance-free.

Plant Selection Criteria

Designers must consider a series of criteria for each plant they select for a garden if it is to thrive and naturally fit in or solve problems. Consider each of these questions to help you to verify that a plant fits the space, works within the overall scheme, and looks great:

- **Height:** Is it tall enough for the job, or is it low enough to avoid blocking your window or crowding an entry in the future?

- **Diameter:** Will it fill the space? Gaps between mature plants can leave some gardens looking bare and empty, but if plants are sized properly your garden will appear full and lush despite drought.

- **Form:** Is the shape of this plant suited to a design solution? Whether columnar, spreading, fountain-shaped, or simply oval, the outline of the plant at maturity is its form. Form is also linked to growth habit so you know what it will do in the future.

- **Exposure:** If the space is in full sun or shade, the plant must prefer it. No matter how beautiful a plant may be, if it's not happy it gets ugly, fast. Know if a plant needs solar protection before you put it on the west side.

- **Winter cold:** Will the plant survive the winter without special protection? Most succulents are not cold hardy except alpines, and many garden-variety African types won't take any frost without damage. Some high-desert species of cacti and succulents such as agaves may prove surprisingly cold hardy. This is important inland from the coast when choosing plants for a long-term landscape.

- **Summer heat:** Will the plant survive a heat wave? Heat in the low desert is quite different than anywhere else, so plants here must stand a month of over 100 degrees F without meltdown, which is what plants do when they give up in desert sun.

- **Water availability:** Is its water need compatible with adjacent plants? You can't drop a desert plant into an existing garden without adjusting irrigation, or it will get too wet. If you can't separate this drought lover from the water lover, one will fail from too much and the other will fail from too little. Irrigation is the big challenge to this whole effort, so you don't kill your new stuff with the same kindness you paid the old standbys.

- **High humidity:** Does high summer humidity cause diseases in that plant? Humidity can cause real problems because soil moisture doesn't evaporate. As a result Mediterraneans and desert species are too easily damaged by rot generated by excessive moisture. The Deep South is plagued with diseases primarily because of the perfectly humid conditions that also help plants flourish there.

- **Low humidity:** Is it adapted to low or absent humidity? When the humidity hovers at the bottom of the scale for months at a time, desert plants thrive while everything else suffers. Spray irrigation has been used in the past, which helped tropicals experience more ambient moisture, but that's not sustainable in drought. Only by planting species that don't demand such humidity will the whole garden become water conservative.

> **TIP:** If you're conscious of global geography, the easiest way to know what plants need is to know where they come from. Sometimes they're grouped to a particular climate region such as "Mediterranean" or they are simply linked to their national origin, such as Australia.

Big Picture: The USDA Plant Hardiness Zone Map

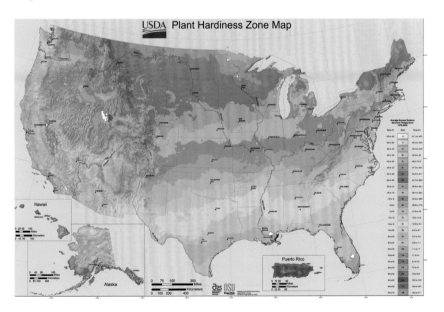

This is the big map of winter cold across the United States. It dictates what grows where based on the average minimum temperature in winter. You can grow a plant in regions warmer than its winter limit, but you can't where it's colder. Botanists have assigned each plant a zone from the map, which you'll often find on plant tags.

However, it's not uncommon to find plants sold without adequate labeling at chain stores. Don't assume they are cold hardy in your area just because they're sold there. Look up the name and find out for sure.

Focus on Your Place: Microclimate

Within a larger climate zone, each homesite becomes an individual environmental space. The lay of the land, the position of the buildings and other improvements, and the way rain falls and whether dew dries quickly in the morning are just a few factors that influence what a plant experiences in its forever home. This variation is most visible in California where conditions can go from alpine to the beach in just a short drive. Where there is such a great deal of variation, the awareness of microclimates is even more vital to plant survival. For example, a low-lying home where cold air drains at night will be much frostier than one on a slope above even though there is no change in zone.

WHERE IS YOUR PLACE?

We can divide most populated areas of the West into a few general geographic categories that have unique characteristics that affect plant growth. Finding where you are in general is important to knowing what kind of challenges and opportunities exist there.

Coasts

All along the Pacific Coast it's the ocean that moderates the weather. The marine influence in low-rainfall regions with very mild winters creates unique growing conditions for certain plants.

Fog: Fog is so prevalent in early summer it's named "June gloom," but it protects plants there from rising inland temperatures. Fog deposits heavy dew in the areas along the coast, which augments limited water supply compared to dry inland areas with the same rainfall.

....

Frost: This is a land of little to no frost in beach towns, then frost potential increases as you head inland.

....

Humidity: High humidity year-round makes coastal living prone to mildew on vulnerable plants, such as certain crape myrtles.

....

UV: Because of the high moisture content in the air, plants are protected from intense sunlight.

....

Wind: Coastal onshore breezes are notorious for tattering large-leaf plants when they are in direct exposure. At certain times off-shore winds coming from the desert stress tender moisture lovers in the airstream.

....

Soils: Salt air can influence sandy soils in beach communities where alkalinity builds up to very high pH with very little microbial activity. Coastal soils can transition to very heavy clay with normal pH but serious drainage issues.

....

Inland Valleys

Throughout the West, inland valleys are warm and mild, though, depending on how far north you are, they can become quite cool in the winter. While most offer optimal agricultural conditions typical of bottomland everywhere, the Great Basin valleys are much drier and should be considered as high desert.

Summer heat: The lack of marine influence creates much drier conditions inland, which require foliage plants adapted to a long dry season such as that of Australia. The combination of wind in summer and fall with high temperatures and low humidity requires supplemental irrigation.

....

Tule fog: Inland valleys can produce tule fog, which does not originate at the beach but is created when moisture and temperatures are just right. It can exist in some areas for weeks at a time, which can try the patience of sun-loving drought-resistant plants.

....

Dry winds: Santa Ana winds come out of the inland deserts, blowing toward the coast. These can be brutally powerful and dry plants out so badly they become volatile.

Ag soils: Our best agricultural soils are on the valley bottomlands beneath twentieth-century housing tracts where conditions are clay and silt, with very high fertility. While just about all plants thrive here, there can be patches of very dense clay that are slow draining. Plants that love lean ground will have problems in such clays, particularly on the valley floor.

....

Mountains

Communities in western mountain ranges experience alpine conditions with long, cold, and very dry winters. Few truly drought-resistant flowering plants survive there, but this is home to low-maintenance high-elevation natives and old-world alpine succulents.

Very cold: Mountain winters are among the coldest in the West, so plants must tolerate heavy snow loads and frozen ground.

....

Late spring: Spring comes late at higher elevations, so plants that flower early in the year may not do well even if they are cold hardy enough.

Lean soils: Backpack anywhere in western ranges and you see a lot of decomposed granite and rock with very granular soils. Greater fertility exists where tree cover is present, but this is still poor ground because of acidic conditions. Compensating with compost and fertilizers may be required.

....

High Desert

The high desert is a land of extremes. In winter it can be bone-chilling cold and in summer intense sunlight drives temperatures high throughout much of the year. Just as such a range is difficult for humans, it's doubly tough on plants since few adapt to both extremes. Because many of the popular desert plants are too tender for high-desert cold, this palette is far more limited than tropical low desert.

High UV: Thin air and lack of humidity means conditions in high desert can be trying for all but the best-adapted species.

....

No humidity: During the summer high-desert conditions can be extremely dry, which is difficult for all but desert-adapted species.

Summer monsoon: Areas influenced by summer moisture from the Gulf of Mexico, such as Arizona, experience summer rainfall and humid conditions. This is a major growing time for native plants in Arizona but elsewhere the effect is humidity without rain.

....

Soils: Desert soils are low in nitrogen and often fast draining except when hardpan is present on the surface or deeper down. Because of fast drainage, irrigation is often more frequent but done for a shorter duration to keep moisture in the root zone long enough to be taken up.

....

Low Desert

Sea-level deserts are somewhat tropical in the Southwest, which is why this is such a winter playground. With limited frost around the first of the year, these are arid zones where a surprising number of plants from tropical climates thrive. Those that do best, however, are from the region of Mexico where they've evolved to withstand the incredible midsummer heat, which can get up to 120 degrees F in July and August.

Very hot summer: Plants unable to take summer heat literally melt in summer even if well watered. Only those that can withstand hot and dry weather make it.

....

Very high UV: With so little atmosphere, low-desert ultraviolet levels are so extreme that plants often physically burn.

....

Mild winter: Without frost, many of the tender arid zone species will do quite well here, and those from other deserts around the world, such as South Africa, will adapt better than in high desert.

....

Super minimal rainfall: There is little to no contribution to plant growth from rains that are too brief and too widely spaced. Desert natives are an exception because they are adapted to a long, dry summer naturally.

....

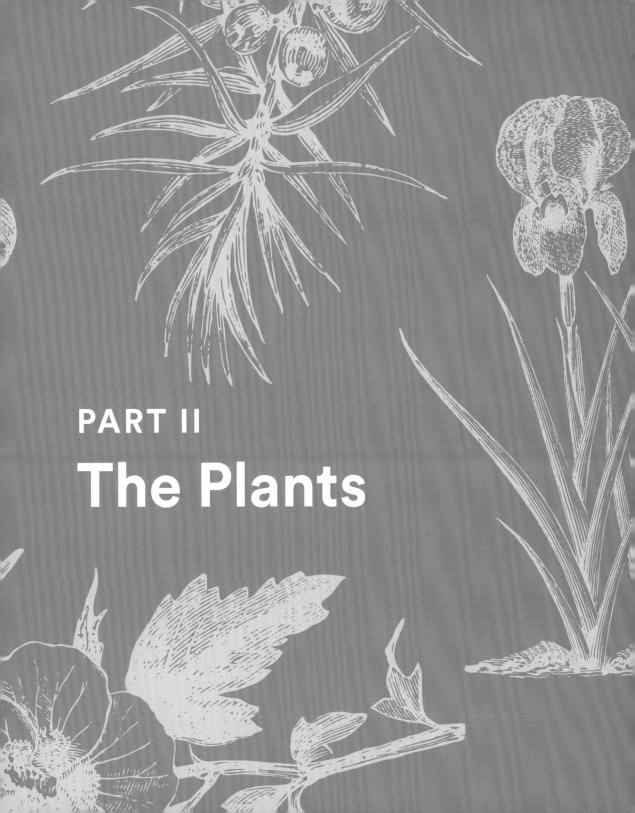

PART II
The Plants

Structure:
Flowering Shrubs

Shrubs are the workhorses of the home landscape. They require little to no care and stand stalwart year after year, improving in size and flowering capability over decades. This longevity makes large shrubs valuable because of the significant time investment to reach full size. Rather than nursing ailing water lovers, replace them with bold flowering alternatives that get bigger and bloom better every year.

In older twentieth-century gardening books, the most popular shrubs of the time were collectively called "deciduous flowering shrubs," which include spiraea, lilac, forsythia, and others. These spring-flowering beauties are also very cold hardy and well adapted to a long icy winter. When they're fully mature the sheer magnitude of color produced by a single large lilac is enough to dominate any spring landscape year after year.

To get this same big color with little water and even less maintenance, strive to plant long-lived woody plants adapted to arid zones. Unlike those deciduous flowering shrubs limited by the short northern growing season, drought-resistant species evolved without such climatic limits. Their flowering season will be much longer, so when a garden is enriched with them, color comes effortlessly.

When Is a Shrub Not a Shrub?
When It's a Big One Pruned as a Tree

"Shrubs" are woody plants, a term applied to all those species with branches and twigs. Shrubs differ from many trees only in size and growth habit. Most produce a very short woody stem that can branch out just inches above the ground or produce a trunk after many years. Often larger shrubs are trained by the grower into a single trunk so the foliage is forced into a canopy, and they're treated as small accent trees.

Monrovia Nursery's introduction, *Rhaphiolepis indica* 'Majestic Beauty', trained to a standard trunk early in life.

Tips on California Native Shrubs

Adding locally native shrubs to your garden is the ideal way to achieve perfect adaptation to your local climate. However, many of them can be a challenge to grow in gardens because of their sensitivity to water in the dry season and insistence on good drainage. Follow these tips to help your native shrubs become established quickly and maximize their drought resistance.

Plant in the fall. The best time to plant in the dry West is in the fall. This gives a young shrub a long, rainy winter to develop new roots that help it face the heat of summer.

....

Water the first summer or two. Natives grown in containers must be supported with careful hand watering the first summer to help them adapt to a new growing ground. Water deeply, then wait until the soil dries out or the growth tips sag before watering again. Do not provide supplemental water after the second growing season.

....

Locate on slopes or higher ground. In the wild, native shrubs tend to dwell on slopes and hills where they are assured good drainage. Choose similar sites in your landscaping or create elevated structures with porous fill to enhance drainage on level ground.

....

Special order. Because of the limited water needs of natives, they rarely survive long in a traditional garden center. Most die of too much water, or moisture applied too frequently or too rarely. It's best to order your natives through your usual garden center and be prepared to pick them up immediately after they come in. This ensures a healthy plant that hasn't been tortured by retail plant care.

....

Wildfire

Many native western shrubs maintain a relationship to wildfire. Ecosystems filled with oil-rich woody shrubs fuel the biggest and most devastating burns. Wildfire is part of the regeneration process of older woody plants that have lost their vigor. They grow decadent with dead or dying wood, and they depend on periodic fire to burn off the aboveground portion of the plant so that new growth can begin from the root crown sequestered safely underground. This demonstrates why a "fire-resistant" shrub actually wants to burn, rather than resisting it as the term suggests. It is resistant simply because it doesn't die. For those in high fire-hazard zones, be aware that should one of these big shrubs catch fire around a home, its flame height will be double that of the plant. Therefore think twice about using taller shrubs near your home and stick to lower-growing woody plants and herbaceous ones in Chapter 4 to maintain defensible space.

Exotic Shrubs

Shrubs from the world's drier climates often share the same oil content as that of California natives. These oils serve a purpose—to replace moisture lost from foliage and wood so the cells won't collapse and kill the plant during extended drought. Many of those from the Mediterranean region are among our best choices for the West Coast because that climate is so similar to ours. The same applies to shrubs from Australia. All of these are far less finicky than the California natives and much easier to grow. They have long been used in western landscaping and will be regular stock at the garden center. Many forms, varieties, and hybrids exist that are widely available, allowing you to choose from many different flower colors rather than that of the original species. When you find success with a shrub such as rosemary, for example, its hybrids allow you to use it in more scenarios because of hybrid changes in size and spread. For example, 'Arp' is a more cold-tolerant form of rosemary for gardens, and 'Barbeque' produces long, straight stems used to make grilling skewers that lend their oils to flavor the meat or vegetables. There's even a low-growing prostrate rosemary used as a groundcover.

Natural Form Is Key to Moisture Retention

One of the most obvious forms of man's dominance over nature is the shearing of naturally shaped shrubs into boxes, balls, and hedges. Hard pruning prevents natural shading of the root zone, a characteristic of the plant's natural shape, which increases drought resistance. It also allows free moisture loss through the open wounds, further reducing resilience. Pruning can also interrupt flower production if done improperly or at the wrong time of year.

Right-Sized Plant for the Space = No Pruning

Radical pruning of shrubs is almost always done for one reason: to reduce the plant's overall size so it fits into the space provided. It's the result of an improperly selected shrub that is too large. This mistake will demand perpetual pruning for the entire life of that shrub. Matching the dimensions of the planting space available to the height and width of your proposed plant is the most important aspect of shrub selection.

TIP: Low branching naturally shades the ground around a shrub to keep its soil and roots cool, reduce moisture evaporation, and discourage competing weeds. To maximize drought resistance, resist the urge to trim, and leave those low branches in place.

The Shrubs

Key

Sun			Bloom Season				Region				
●	◑	○	✤	☀	🍂	❄	HD	LD	M	C	IV
SHADE	PARTLY SUNNY	SUN	SPRING	SUMMER	FALL	WINTER	HIGH DESERT	LOW DESERT	MOUN-TAINS	COAST	INLAND VALLEY

CALLIANDRA

These natives are called "fairy dusters" because these delightful shrubs produce small powder-puff flowers composed of densely packed pink or reddish stamens. The foliage is fine and fernlike, though it can be sparse in high heat of the desert summer. When in bloom they grant a beautiful haze of color that's intense in late spring, then continues intermittently over many months, stimulated by moisture of drip irrigation or monsoon thunderstorms. Irresistible to hummingbirds, this shrub is essential habitat garden material. Sadly these shrubs are too often sheared, which sacrifices their natural airy flowering growth for a dense mass, spoiling their beauty in the garden setting. There are only two species widely cultivated, both ideal for the hot inland valleys and low desert, one cold-hardy enough for the high desert. 'Sierra Star' is a new hybrid of both these species that blooms bright red all year round and may soon prove to be superior to its parents in both color and adaptability.

Calliandra californica (Baja Fairy Duster)

Height	Width	Zone	Sun	Bloom Season		Region		Flower Color
6'	5'	9	○	✤	☀	LD	C	Red

Calliandra eriophylla (Fairy Duster)

Height	Width	Zone	Sun	Bloom Season	Region			Flower Color
3'	3'	7	O	✿	HD	LD	IV	Pink

Calliandra californica (Baja Fairy Duster)

Bottom left and right: *Calliandra eriophylla* (Fairy Duster)

CALLISTEMON

Callistemon citrinus (Bottlebrush)

Height	Width	Zone	Sun		Bloom Season			Region			Flower Color
10'–20'	10'–15'	9	◑	○	✿	☀	⚜	LD	C	IV	Red

Around the mid-twentieth century, fast-growing Australian bottlebrush burst into western landscapes as one of the signature species of the modern postwar tract house. Popular in low-water areas of Southern California, it became the symbol of the carefree ease of the Pacific Coast lifestyle. This is one of those shrubs that can easily grow up to tree-sized proportions. It's also an example of one shrub that can benefit from natural pruning. If left to its own devices *Callistemon* develops a large foliage mass that doesn't do its growth habit justice. When the interior is thinned out the structure and the curious woody seedpods are revealed. Pods can remain on branches for decades waiting for a wildfire to heat and release seed. One of the early mistakes in midcentury landscapes is using this plant more than once or twice on any site—it's just that dominant with all that vivid red color. But for red lovers, it's a blaze of glory in bloom that's outstanding in sun or under night lighting.

CASSIA

Height	Width	Zone	Sun	Bloom Season	Region		Flower Color
3'–8'	3'–6'	9	O	✿	LD	IV	Yellow

These golden-yellow flowering Australian natives are not only standouts when in spring bloom; they make an exceptional effect when combined with blue or purple flowering companions. For the rest of the year their gray-green feathery foliage is a lovely, light-filled textural accent. They love the heat and full sun and are remarkably tolerant of problem soils with little fertility and rapid drainage. In the wild they prefer sites on slopes and ridges, wherever the root zone is free enough to drain quickly. This shrub has proven itself in the rigors of the low-desert furnace and that makes it a problem solver for hot spots and rough ground too challenging for other, hungrier plants. Their only drawback is limited frost hardiness to about 28 degrees F, which prevents their use in the higher foothills and high desert.

Cassia artemisioides (Feathery Cassia)

Botanical Name	Common Name	Height	Diameter	Foliage
Cassia artemisioides	Feathery Cassia	3'–5'	3'–5'	Fine
Cassia nemophila	Desert Cassia	5'–8'	4'–6'	Fine
Cassia phyllodinea	Silvery Cassia	3'–5'	4'–6'	Coarse

CEANOTHUS

Height	Width	Zone	Sun		Bloom Season	Region			Flower Color
3'–10'	5'–12'	7–8	◑	○	✿	M	C	IV	Blue

The rarest flower color in the drought-tolerant garden is a true blue, which is why the *Ceanothus* shrubs are so beloved by westerners. With forty species native to California and adjacent states, *Ceanothus* shrubs are suited to virtually every microclimate except the desert. Yet few are in the nurseries because these shrubs are highly sensitive to overwatering, particularly in combination with heavy soils and relatively level ground. In the wild these species prefer cliff faces, slopes, and high spots where moisture never accumulates for long. This makes them difficult for growers because of such finicky water requirements, and garden center retailers are loathe to stock them because of the great potential for losses. Over the last 50 years breeders have crossed the most adaptable species with those bearing the most prolific or large flowers to create more garden varieties.

Ceanothus Cultivar Selection Matrix

These hybrid varieties have been in cultivation for decades and have proved themselves in western landscaping. They are widely available and, with many different sizes, there is a suitable replacement for any traditional shrub.

Variety	Height	Diameter	Flower Color	Foliage
'Concha'	5'–7'	6'–10'	Cobalt blue	Glossy
'Dark Star'	4'–6'	5'–6'	Deep blue	Tiny
'Frosty Blue'	8'–10'	10'–12'	Medium blue	Glossy
'Joyce Coulter'	3'–5'	8'–10'	Medium blue	Dark green
'Julia Phelps'	5'–6'	6'–8'	Purple blue	Small
'Ray Hartman'	15'	10'–15'	Medium blue	Dark glossy

CISTUS

Cistus purpureus (Orchid Rockrose)

Height	Width	Zone	Sun	Bloom Season	Region			Flower Color
3'–5'	3'–5'	6	O	❀	HD	C	IV	Pink

Rockrose is to the wildlands of southern Europe what sagebrush is to the western states. This redolent shrub was valued in ancient times for its oils, which became coveted in the perfume trade where it was known as "labdanum." Desire to cultivate it farther north led to much breeding a century ago, but today just a few species and varieties are used for the landscape. Orchid rockrose has been the primary species for use in landscaping in very hot, dry locations, slopes, and rock gardens. It is not finicky about soils except in low, poorly drained locations. These shrubs thrive and bloom best where summers are long and dry. Because this is a native of North Africa and southern Europe, it's adapted to cool, rainy winters and hot, dry summers, which is a perfect fit for Mediterranean climates. Another species, the crimson-spot rockrose, is not so widely planted but is an excellent problem solver for places where afternoon sun and reflected heat of paving are too daunting for other plants. *Cistus ladanifer* blooms white, is 5 to 7 feet tall, and is considered the most heat and drought tolerant of the larger species. All thrive in the heat of inland valleys, sun-drenched foothills, and high desert, and yet they're equally successful in coastal areas farther south.

FREMONTODENDRON

Fremontodendron californicum (Flannel Bush)

Height	Width	Zone	Sun	Bloom Season	Region			Flower Color
10'–20'	10'–15'	9	O	✿	M	C	IV	Yellow

In the Sierra Nevada foothills, the only place you'll see a flannel bush in the wild is high on a south-facing slope demonstrating a preference for extreme drainage and all-day sun without too much exposure in the late afternoon. They pop out on the tail end of winter, covered in golden-yellow blooms while conditions are still cool and moist. The species can grow to a large size in the coastal ranges. Breeders have created a number of hybrids that bear much larger flowers better suited to smaller gardens. 'California Glory' is among the most widely grown. These shrubs are rarely kept in stock at the garden center, but they're easily available via special order.

Beware that flannel bush can be challenging to grow for the novice because of its preference for very dry summer conditions, but once established it proves one of the most carefree and beautiful of all native flowering shrubs. Use them in landscapes along the coast and inland valleys as well as mountain foothills of the southern ranges.

HETEROMELES

Heteromeles arbutifolia (Christmas Berry, Toyon)

Height	Width	Zone	Sun	Bloom Season	Region			Flower Color
10'	8'	8	⭘	✿	HD	M	IV	White

Toyon is without question the most important yet underrecognized evergreen native shrub of California. Tough, extremely drought resistant, and hardy to 0 degrees F, it is the ideal choice for mountains, high desert, and colder inland valleys but is most at home in the foothills. Though the small white flowers are not particularly showy except under a full moon, it's the red berries that follow that highlight the dormant winter landscape in the West. Its common name Christmas berry describes its early popularity as a holiday decorating plant. Each year migrating robins will lay over in areas where the plants are numerous to feed on the red berries, making this an important species for wildlife. In the wild these shrubs are often seen along highways at hillsides and cut slopes where their abnormally deep roots provide excellent anchorage on rugged sites.

HIBISCUS

Hibiscus syriacus (Rose of Sharon)

Height	Width	Zone	Sun		Bloom Season	Region			Flower Color	Type
10'	6'	5	◑	○	☀	M	C	IV	Pink, white, lavender, blue	Deciduous

We don't expect to find hibiscus among drought-resistant plants, yet an old favorite in parts of arid Texas and California has become better than ever by breeding. Rose of Sharon is counted among the traditional deciduous flowering shrubs, but this is a midsummer bloomer valued in the season when little else shows color. In some cases they continue to bloom sparsely through to the end of fall. Rose of Sharon is deciduous, upright growing, and can reach large proportions. These beautiful shrubs produce big hibiscus-type flowers that can lend a tropical look or add romance to a cottage garden. The most reliable are bred by the US National Arboretum for increased tolerance of heat, drought, and poor soils, plus they bloom longer and are disease resistant. Its resilience makes this an ideal shrub for mountains and inland valleys where it tolerates frost to 0 degrees F and snow.

US National Arboretum Introductions— *Hibiscus syriacus* Hybrids

Variety	Height	Diameter	Flower Color
'Aphrodite'	9'	7'	Pink, red
'Diana'	8'	7'	White
'Helene'	8'	6'	White, red
'Minerva'	8'	6'	Lavender, pink, red

LAVATERA

Lavatera maritima (Tree Mallow)

Height	Width	Zone	Sun	Bloom Season	Region		Flower Color
6'–8'	8'–12'	9	O	✿	C	IV	Lavender purple

This is a fast-growing spreading shrub that is quintessentially West Coast and provides a romantic cottage garden feel. It's a native of the Mediterranean basin, from North Africa across to southern France and westward into Spain where conditions are hot and dry. The flowers offer a lovely two-tone soft pink blossom shaped much like a smallish hibiscus that lends an airy, cooling feel to outdoor living spaces. It's a prolific bloomer flowering in early spring, followed by intermittent flushes stimulated by water applications. The large upright form makes for a bold accent or a single background. This shrub has proven its mettle from the rigors of the low desert, but it thrives along the coast and in milder inland valleys. Its only drawback is sensitivity to cold and wind, so its ideal location will be in spaces protected from exposure and frost. Like so many fast-growing woody plants, this shrub may suffer shortened longevity to as little as 5 years, but this may be due to extreme conditions.

LEPTOSPERMUM

Leptospermum scoparium (New Zealand Tea Tree)

Height	Width	Zone	Sun	Bloom Season	Region			Flower Color
10'	10'	9	O	✿	M	C	IV	Red

The common name for this shrub comes from its value on board South Pacific sailing vessels where it was brewed into tea that alleviated scurvy on long sea voyages. The original species was white-flowered and not particularly showy, but the early cultivars were avidly adopted along the coast. Very old specimens of 'Ruby Glow' can be seen all over California in Victorian neighborhoods, but tragically many have been sheared beyond all recognition. A beautiful open branching structure would be far more attractive if left to its own devices. This is a big plant overall, ranging from 5 to 12 feet tall. The small flowers about the size of a quarter are so numerous the entire shrub becomes one solid mass of color with spring flowering. It is indeed intense enough to compete with vivid bougainvillea. Tea tree is best planted as a single specimen with a lot of space to allow for its natural form, or it may be pruned up from the ground for a more treelike appearance. Avoid planting close to a pool or upwind from one, as the leaves and flowers are so tiny they can't be skimmed and must be vacuumed.

LEUCOPHYLLUM

Height	Width	Zone	Sun	Bloom Season		Region			Flower Color
4'–8'	4'–8'	8	O	⬡	⚘	HD	LD	IV	Blue, purple

Few shrubs can match the standout beauty of those known collectively as Texas ranger. The many varieties offer flower shades from intense blue to purples. They are long-blooming, from an intense spring flush to intermittent flowers from late spring into fall. These Texas native shrubs are unbelievably tolerant of very high-desert heat, but they are not necessarily desert plants. They prefer lean limestone soils, which makes them a good fit for slopes and cuts where drainage is assured, or in rock gardens where the root crown is well above the surrounding grade. These shrubs are not tolerant of heavy soils and perpetual moisture, so they are not recommended for the immediate coast. However, the farther inland they grow, the larger and more floriferous they become. They can be divided into more silvery foliage varieties and green-leaf cultivars, each offering a very different appeal when not in bloom. Because of the wide range of sizes, it's important to choose the one that fits best, as they too often outgrow their space and must be radically pruned. Reserve them for your problem hot spots and areas that suffer from reflected heat in the summer months.

Leucophyllum laevigatum (Texas Ranger)

Texas Ranger Species for Landscaping

The best of the Texas rangers for landscaping fall under these three most well-known species, although there are others. Note that *L. candidum* is the most sensitive to overwatering. The green foliage types offer a more lush appearance but the silvery pubescent forms are more visually appealing in flower gardens, as they are similar in color to the artemisias and brittlebushes.

Species/Variety	Flowers	Foliage	Height	Diameter
Leucophyllum candidum 'Silver Cloud'	Violet	Silvery	4'–5'	4'–5'
Leucophyllum frutescens 'Green Cloud'	Deep violet	Green	6'–8'	6'–8'
Leucophyllum laevigatum	Blue purple	Green	4'–5'	4'–5'

TECOMA

Tecoma stans hybrids (Yellow Bells)

Height	Width	Zone	Sun	Bloom Season			Region		Flower Color
5'–12'	5'–8'	10–11	O	✿	☀	🌿	LD	IV	Yellow, orange

Big, bold trumpet-shaped flowers come nonstop from late spring to the holidays, making *Tecoma* hybrids the highlight of the warm season garden. It's truly amazing the amount of flowers these plants produce every day, and they are so vigorous the lush green foliage quickly develops into a sizable plant even when planted in summer heat, growing 12 to 25 feet tall, so it's almost a tree at maturity. Humming-birds and mason bees love the nectar,

and rabbits eat the fallen blossoms. The species is not frost hardy and considered tropical, and although the foliage may die back from frost, the root crown is more cold tolerant and will replace foliage the following summer. In habitat it's found in full sun and the sandy ground of dry washes all over the Southwest, Texas, and into Mexico, where they thrive in the heat and root deeply to access moisture hidden underground, which is what makes them so incredibly drought resistant. In recent years the yellow-flowered species, *Tecoma stans*, has been crossed with other wild species to increase both cold hardiness and flower color range. Plants will become partially deciduous in warm climates, but where it's cold they are fully deciduous during the winter. Cut back in late spring for tidier strength and form. They are summer standouts throughout the neighborhood when little else is in bloom. While this shrub has long been in desert gardens, it deserves a special place in the arid palette of colorful bloomers everywhere else there's drought because of the increased cold hardiness of the hybrids.

Top *Tecoma* Hybrids for Landscapes

Variety	Flower	Frost	Height	Diameter
Tecoma stans var. *angustata*	Yellow	5 degrees F	5'–6'	5'–6'
'Gold Star'	Yellow	20 degrees F	8'	8'
'Orange Jubilee'	Orange	10 degrees F	12'	8'
'Crimson Flare'	Red	15 degrees F	6'–8'	6'–8'
'Sierra Apricot'	Peach	15 degrees F	3'	4'–5'
'Solar Flare'	Tangerine	15 degrees F	4'–6'	4'–6'
'Sunrise'	Copper	10 degrees F	8'	8'

Five Flowering Shrubs That Take a Frost

1. *Ceanothus* spp. (California Lilac)

2. *Cistus* spp. and hybrids (Rockrose)

3. *Heteromeles arbutifolia* (Christmas Berry, Toyon)

4. *Hibiscus syriacus* (Rose of Sharon)

5. *Tecoma stans* hybrids (Yellow Bells)

Five Summer and Late-Summer Bloomers

1. *Calliandra* spp. (Fairy Duster)

2. *Cassia* spp. (Senna)

3. *Hibiscus syriacus* (Rose of Sharon)

4. *Lavatera maritima* (Tree Mallow)

5. *Tecoma stans* hybrids (Yellow Bells)

Five High-Heat–Tolerating Shrubs

1. *Calliandra* spp. (Fairy Duster)

2. *Cassia* spp. (Senna)

3. *Callistemon citrinus* (Bottlebrush)

4. *Leucophyllum* spp. (Texas Ranger)

5. *Tecoma stans* hybrids (Yellow Bells)

Shrubs Selection Matrix

BOTANICAL NAME	COMMON NAME	ZONE	COLOR
Calliandra californica*	Baja Fairy Duster	9	Red
Calliandra eriophylla	Fairy Duster	7	Pink
Calliandra 'Sierra Star'	Sierra Star Fairy Duster	9	Red
Callistemon citrinus	Bottlebrush	9	Red
Cassia spp.	Senna	9	Yellow
Ceanothus hybrids*	California Lilac	7–8	Blue
Cistus purpureus	Orchid Rockrose	6	Pink
Fremontodendron californicum	Flannel Bush	9	Yellow
Heteromeles arbutifolia*	Christmas Berry, Toyon	8	Red berries
Hibiscus syriacus	Rose of Sharon	5	Varies
Lavatera maritime	Tree Mallow	9	Lavender purple
Leptospermum scoparium	New Zealand Tea Tree	9	Red
Leucophyllum spp.	Texas Ranger	8	Blue, purple
Tecoma stans hybrids*	Yellow Bells	10–11	Yellow, orange

*Indicates California native species.

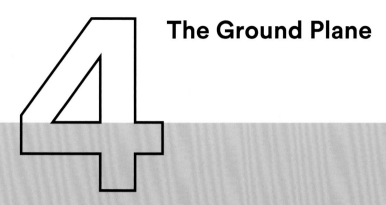

The Ground Plane

Drought is driving a whole new approach to space in the residential landscape. In times past, designers used lawns to fill open space and cover the ground plane with cool green grass. They provided a place to play and relax for both humans and pets. Today lawns are disappearing as homeowners realize that the water, chemicals, and maintenance required to care for a lawn are not sustainable on any level. The result is the creation of new ground plane treatments that utilize both hard materials and specialized plants.

So What Is a Ground Plane?

Designers refer to the surface of the ground as the ground plane of your home-site. Consider it equivalent to the subfloor of your home that's topped with carpet or tile or wood flooring depending on the use of the room. The ground plane of every homesite is just as important, and efforts are made to find alternatives to turf grass "carpets" that are appealing to homeowners. Today sustainable ground plane treatments focus on surfaces that demand little to no moisture, allow for moisture to percolate down to the water table, and maintain an attractive appearance overall. The contemporary style is a blend of gravels, paving, and low-spreading plants to create a mosaic of interest where that greedy lawn once filled the space.

Step-by-Step Design in Lieu of Lawns

When ditching the lawn, or at least part of it, use this process to help you create a new useful and beautiful space that perfectly suits your family's needs.

Step 1 **Assess your future use of the space.** This requires you to think deeply about how you will use the ground plane formerly covered with lawn. Here are a list of possibilities: dining patio, veggie garden, pet enclosure or small lawn, sports courts, mounded succulent garden, or a spa with privacy planting. Make a list of possibilities for your project, then you can start prioritizing them.

TIP: To get a real feel of how much space your lawn covers and what you can do there, use white kitchen flour and a tape measure to see what fits before you strip out the lawn. Literally lay the flour out on top of mud or grass, and you can even put a table out there to see if it fits with chairs. This takes all the risk out of the design process because you know it will fit. To make a correction, just wash or brush the flour away and redraw.

Step 2 **Determine the size of spaces you want to create.** In general designers know the minimum dimensions required for outdoor living spaces are rarely smaller than 10 by 10 feet and usually larger. This is important if you are going to use flagstone or precast concrete slabs with gapped joints for drainage. You need plenty of room to get all four chair legs to be on solid ground. Often by the time this is resolved there's not a lot of room left for plants.

Step 3 **Evaluate what you see from indoors and where you want the eye to go.**
Designers always draw doors and windows of the house on their plan so we know
what the owner sees when they look outside. This helps you know where the focal
points are or should be within that space. Pay special attention to often-used window
views such as over the kitchen sink or from the master bedroom, which are often
neglected in favor of the bigger sliding doors at the living room or family room.

Step 4 **Connect spaces and pathways with existing circulation.** These connections
must be intuitive and meet existing points exactly so the new space integrates seam-
lessly with your existing paving and sidewalks. These paths should be wide enough
to move a wheelbarrow through without crowding. They should be clear of spiny
plants and follow your intuition. Avoid corners where people cut through where
they aren't supposed to walk, which is evidenced by kids and dogs. Work with them,
not against them, or you'll fight it forever.

Step 5 **Create small spaces for plants.** The old way of adding plants was to create big
planters and fill them up. Now with spot irrigation you can use plants anywhere in
the space, so don't feel you must have traditional ones. Succulents and specimens
in gravel fields can be stunning alone in a simple composition for truly excellent
night-lighting opportunities. For widespread plant locations, bury mainline drip
tubing before laying gravel, then hook it up after as plants go in.

Step 6 **Use individual accents for fun and excitement.** Don't succumb to the barren
look when there are so many ways to liven up a dry garden. With so little water
delivered, materials hold up longer in the elements. These need not be a particular
style but one that appeals to your own sense of beauty and functionality. Perhaps
you have a sculpture or boulders or driftwood or other outdoor accents that make an
ideal centerpiece for succulents and grasses.

Creeping Shrubs

Creeping shrubs are low maintenance, long-lived, and easily irrigated. Growing different species in a patchwork results in beautiful contrasts in foliage and flower color over large areas formerly devoted to lawns. Because of the wide range of coverage diameters, there are perfect fits for virtually any scenario in any climate. Though slower to become established, they are worth the wait for many years of carefree beauty.

Key

Sun			Bloom Season				Region				
●	◑	○	✽	☀	🍁	❄	HD	LD	M	C	IV
SHADE	PARTLY SUNNY	SUN	SPRING	SUMMER	FALL	WINTER	HIGH DESERT	LOW DESERT	MOUN-TAINS	COAST	INLAND VALLEY

ARCTOSTAPHYLOS

Height	Width	Zone	Sun		Bloom Season	Region				Flower Color
1'–4'	4'–12'	7–8	◑	○	✽	HD	M	C	IV	Pink, white

The manzanitas are shrubs that include a few creeping forms widely used in landscaping. Dense habit, dark green color, and remarkable drought resistance has made them popular lawn substitutes. You'll love the heather-like tiny bell-shaped pink or white flowers that taste like honey. Finicky about location, drainage, and water, they can naturalize once established when the rains return. Most are hardy to Zones 7 and 8. *Arctostaphylos uva-ursi* is an exception, hardy to Zone 3 and ideally suited to dry mountains and middle-elevation foothills throughout the West.

CEANOTHUS

Height	Width	Zone	Sun		Bloom Season	Region			Flower Color
3'–10'	5'–12'	7–8	◑	○	✣	M	C	IV	Blue

California lilacs are one of the most beautiful genera of native shrubs. The shiny emerald-green foliage offers a lush appearance accented by vivid blue flowers in spring on the growth tips. Prostrate forms are a lawn substitute. Inland the most important species is *Ceanothus griseus* var. *horizontalis*, Zone 8, which spreads to 12 feet in diameter with a height ranging from 2 to 3 feet. It has proven its adaptability to a wide range of conditions and is not quite so finicky about summer water. On the coast the preferable species is *Ceanothus maritimus*, which ranges from 1 to 3 feet tall, spreading to 6 feet in diameter. This species thrives in the maritime coastal garden and easily naturalizes there but will not prove vigorous inland.

Plant	Diameter	Height	Zone	Foliage
Ceanothus griseus var. *horizontalis*	12'	2'–3'	8	Glossy
Ceanothus maritimus	6'	1'–3'	8	Tiny

CISTUS

Height	Width	Zone	Sun	Bloom Season	Region			Flower Color
12"–24"	6'–8'	8	O	✿	HD	C	IV	White, pink

Mediterranean rockroses include two excellent spreading shrubs that provide both rough aromatic foliage and bright spring color. *Cistus salvifolius* 'Prostratus' is a white-flowered form that produces copious early spring blooms. The more popular *Cistus* 'Sunset' is a very showy hybrid bearing magenta-rose–colored flowers with bright yellow centers. This is a groundcover form of the shrubby orchid rockrose to extend its coloring into low, broad expanses. This is a great plant for slopes and rocky outcrops where the aromatic scents from its oil-rich leaves will be released into the air for a truly Mediterranean experience. Oil of rockrose was coveted by the ancient Egyptians for cosmetics and aromatherapy.

Cistus 'Sunset'

Plant	Diameter	Height	Zone	Foliage
Cistus salvifolius 'Prostratus'	6'	24"	8	Pubescent
Cistus 'Sunset'	8'	12"	8	Tiny

DALEA

Dalea greggii (Trailing Indigo Bush)

Height	Width	Zone	Sun	Bloom Season		Region	Flower Color
8"–12"	4'–6'	10	O	✿	☀	LD	Violet blue

Known as trailing indigo bush in its desert habitat, fine-textured gray-leaf *Dalea greggii* is a relative of the amazing desert smoke tree, *Dalea spinosa*. Both bear the very same iridescent violet-blue flowers in the dead heat of early summer. It's a fast-growing mat-like spreading evergreen shrub that rarely exceeds a foot in height, spreading 4 to 6 feet or more. This is a superior problem solver for frost-free very dry conditions and alkaline soils. *Dalea* is sensitive to root rot when overwatered in the heat, so save it for hell strips along the driveway or hot west-facing slopes, and let it cascade off the face of retaining walls. *Dalea* is frost sensitive although there is some evidence it may tolerate temperatures as low as 25 degrees F.

LANTANA

Lantana montevidensis hybrids

Height	Width	Zone	Sun	Bloom Season				Region		Flower Color
12"–18"	4'–10'	10	O	⊛	☀	🍁	❄	LD	C	Purple, yellow, others

If not cut back by frost, *Lantana* remains in a perpetual state of bloom much of the year. Certain hybrids and species make outstanding spreading plants that offer bold color where few other bloomers can take the heat. There are many hybrids of *L. montevidensis*, the species that bears rich lavender blooms for a solid mass of color in very low-growing plants that spread over very large areas. Breeding has produced "spreading" hybrids such as 'Cream Carpet', 'Spreading Sunshine', and 'Spreading Sunset' that grow to 18 inches tall, spreading 4 to 6 feet across for bold masses of long-lasting yellow and orange. Outstanding results occur when you blend the lavender species with the 'Spreading Sunshine' hybrid for bold color contrast. *Lantana* copes with extreme drought by temporarily defoliating partially or completely, and it may prove able to return from winter frost so long as the main stem and roots survive. There is no better plant to liven up gravel gardens for a single year or many, depending on the local climate and rainfall.

ROSMARINUS

Rosmarinus officinalis 'Prostratus'

Height	Width	Zone	Sun	Bloom Season		Region					Flower Color
6"	5'	8	O	✿	☀	HD	LD	M	C	IV	Blue

Traditional rosemary includes a single low-growing variety, *Rosmarinus officinalis* 'Prostratus', which proves to be among the most heat- and drought-tolerant spreading shrubs. A staple of Mediterranean gardens, this creeper is famous for cascading off retaining walls, rock curbs, and slopes. Beautiful blue flowers on the dark forest-green field are a cooling accent for very hot sites. Slow-growing, this shrub also provides an endless source of seasoning for the kitchen.

Herbaceous Groundcovers

Herbaceous plants are composed entirely of soft tissues and lack woody parts. The problem with herbaceous groundcovers is these masses of foliage and flowers require many individuals to provide coverage. Once Bermuda grass, oxalis, or other pernicious weeds become established among the plants, it can be nearly impossible to permanently clean them out. However, when herbaceous groundcovers are planted in small patches rather than large areas, weeds are more easily managed. And if you get a weed infestation that is not resolvable, simply remove the "patch" entirely and start over.

The second issue with herbaceous groundcovers is water applications. With so many individual plants it's hard to water them all adequately without spray irrigation. This requires a complex drip system to feed large areas because drip is not designed for broadcast water applications, and if there are any malfunctioning emitters the groundcovers will brown out there. For smaller patches drip easily adapts with micro-spray emitters that broadcast over a foot-diameter space ideal for these limited plantings.

ARCTOTIS

Arctotis acaulis hybrids (African Daisy)

Height	Width	Zone	Sun	Bloom Season		Region			Flower Color
12"	12"–18"	9	○	⌘	☀	LD	C	IV	Many

The quintessential midcentury groundcover for modern tract homes in the West were gazanias and *Osteospermum*, also known as "freeway daisy." Because they lack longevity, none of these have maintained popularity in contemporary dry gardens. Instead the popular hybrid is a great new plant bred by Australians using species of the South African native *Arctotis*. What makes them such outstanding plants for color patches is their intensely bright flower hues well beyond that of their osteo-gazania predecessors. *Arctotis* hybrids produce dense, fuzzy gray foliage with a big bloom season followed by spotty flowering. Their Achilles' heel is a lack of frost tolerance, which limits them to about 25 degrees F, but if frosted back they may regrow from the roots the following season. There is no better plant for slopes, pockets in rocky outcrops, and swaths of incredible color for gardens large and small.

THYMUS

Thymus serpyllum (Creeping Thyme)

Height	Width	Zone	Sun		Bloom Season	Region				Flower Color
4"	12"	4	◑	○	✿	HD	LD	C	IV	Pink

TIP: In hot climates, growing tiny plants between flagstones that absorb incredible heat during the day is a real challenge. Most plants require underground in-line drip irrigation to survive. High-quality artificial turf makes a far better porous filler for flagstones that requires no care or water and looks cool and lush all year round.

Until recently creeping thyme was found only in herb gardens, but today it's a favorite filler between flagstones. It is native to the Mediterranean where these aromatic ground-hugging spreaders grow wild on sun-drenched rocky areas and in the sandy soils of the coastal bluffs. This is a drought-resistant plant that is highly sensitive to excessive moisture and poor drainage. Inland and in the desert it does best under bright filtered sun and away from direct afternoon exposure. These mats are beautiful in bloom and make a fine choice for rock gardens and difficult spots too porous for other plants. Many different varieties of creeping thyme offer a range of foliage hues and vivid flower colors.

VINCA

Vinca major, Vinca minor (Common Periwinkle)

Height	Width	Zone	Sun			Bloom Season	Region			Flower Color
5"–12"	2'–3', spreading farther	7	●	◐	○	✿	M	C	IV	Blue

In the far West, it's not uncommon to find this plant naturalized in shady pioneer graveyards, proving its adaptability to extended drought. The fast-growing genus produces the standard *Vinca major*, which is larger but visually identical to its small-leaf, flatter cousin, *V. minor*. Variegated forms exist for both large and small species. Cold hardy to Zone 7, they produce a beautiful periwinkle-blue flower that is delicate-looking for such a rugged plant. This is an exceptional choice for beneath shade trees to create a lush, weed-blocking carpet. When *Vinca* becomes old and decadent, it tolerates radical trimming or mowing to renew the foliage and stimulate more flowering.

SUCCULENT CARPETS

"Iceplant" is a general term for all succulent groundcovers. In the 1960s, *Carpobrotus edulis*, the first and most invasive of all iceplants, was a freeway erosion control favorite. It is so drought resistant that it has invaded many coastal habitats, displacing important native species in the dune communities. However, invasiveness inland may be limited by very low humidity and high heat, where spread may be checked by extreme drought and absence of marine influence.

The remaining species of iceplant produce denser, almost Day-Glo flowers, creating an intense mass in full bloom. In the Desert Garden of the Huntington Library in San Marino, a wide range of these iceplant groundcovers are well established. There you'll see just how many different colored varieties exist among these primary species and their variants.

Succulent iceplant adds color to open spaces, gravel gardens, and hot spots on the coast. These are also perfect problem solvers for shallow soils, rocky outcrops, and slopes too challenging for other plants. The trick is selecting the right one for your microclimate because they do vary considerably in frost tolerance.

Plant	Zone	Common Name
Carpobrotus edulis	7	Iceplant
Cephalophyllum speciosum	10	Red Spike Iceplant
Delosperma cooperi	8	Iceplant
Lampranthus spectabilis	9	Trailing Iceplant

Delosperma cooperi

Exotic iceplant

Lampranthus spectabilis

Carpobrotus edulis

Carpobrotus sp.

Hardscape: Bark and Plastic Failed

During the last great California drought in the 1970s, homeowners were replacing lawns for much the same reason we do today. Back then the grass was replaced by black plastic sheeting covered with ground bark. Drought-resistant plants were then planted through holes made in the plastic. Over time problems cropped up:

- Plastic cut off oxygen to the soil, causing it to sour and lose microbes and fertility.

- Plastic degraded under sunlight to break down into millions of smaller pieces.

- Plastic prevented rainwater from entering the soil.

- Bark often floated away during heavy rains.

- Weeds (often lawn grasses such as Bermuda) cropped up through planting holes.

TRY THIS INSTEAD: WEED BARRIER AND GRAVEL

What is weed barrier? Heavy-duty synthetic woven materials generally called geotextiles resist decomposition and provide a long-lasting sheeting to separate gravel mulches from the soil underneath. Quality weed barrier can be expected to maintain its integrity for 20 years. This material is dense enough to block light and prevent weed seed germination. It's porous enough to allow water and air to be exchanged in both directions. These characteristics make it ideal for improving the long-term success of alternatives to the traditional lawn:

- Weed barrier allows oxygen to move through for soil health.

- Weed barrier allows rain to penetrate to reach soil.

- Weed barrier is woven and does not break down in sunlight.

- Gravel doesn't float away in heavy rains.

- Gravel is available in many sizes and colors, not just bark brown.

- Gravel blends with stone paving and landscape boulders for more natural planting.

Material Close Up: Gravel

Gravel is proving one of the most popular alternatives to lawn, and in some cases it's also replacing paving so that rain and irrigation water can more easily percolate down into the soil rather than run off into the storm drain. In the process of making changes to your landscape for improved drought resistance, it's important to use the right gravel for that unique site.

Size: Gravel varies by the size of each particle. For example, pea gravel averages about ¼ inch. The smaller the particles the easier and safer it is to walk on and rake out. You can't rake larger gravel. Larger particle sizes allow gradual accumulation of dirt and organic matter, which fosters a haven for weed seeds to sprout. Finer gravels are less prone to this problem and choosing one that's easy to rake clean after fall leaf drop or a summer storm will make long-term maintenance a snap.

Origins: Gravel is heavy to haul and when it originates close to home it's cheaper to produce and haul. Beware of gravel that originates far away because hauling charges to the local distributor and then to your site can become astronomical for an otherwise low-cost bulk material.

Color: In general, earth tones and gray tones tend to be the swankiest looks for landscaping. With darker gravel, bits of sun-bleached organic matter accumulate and stand out in high contrast. Black and steel-gray gravel also absorbs a tremendous amount of heat during the day, which may disturb nearby plants. In addition, the release of this heat in the evening into the adjacent outdoor living spaces may be undesirable. Lighter earth tones tolerate organic matter beautifully and lend a beautiful light background for plants.

Crushed: Decorative rocks are often mined and crushed to create beautiful gravel. The quarry separates out the crushed gravel into uniform sizes. This allows you to use the same surfacing material in different sizes on the same site to create textural variations in the ground plane without color changes. Crushed gravel has sharp edges that dig into moist ground to hold tightly so it won't travel on slight inclines.

....

River run: Pebbles from shores of the waterways and rivers feature a uniformly rounded appearance. They're easier on bare feet too. However, rounded pebbles travel easily by rolling downhill, which also makes them tricky for people wearing high heels or for unsteady seniors. River run gravels are best used in small, flat spaces and for creating dry streambeds where they are a natural fit.

....

FIRE SAFETY: GROUND PLANE PLANTING AND DEFENSIBLE SPACE

Fire is always more dangerous in drought and dry areas. As author of California's first book on wildfire landscaping decades ago, I set forth the criteria for planting for low fuel volumes in high fire-hazard zones. Fuel volume is simply the amount of flammable material a single plant presents to the oncoming fire.

What makes this so important is this fact: the flame will always be twice the height of the plant. This is why low-growing ground plane plants in this chapter are so important. A foot-tall spreading shrub makes a 2-foot flame, which is easy to suppress compared to a 3-foot shrub that supports a man-sized flame.

Fire can travel only where there is fuel. The defensible space landscape is composed of low-spreading plants separated by spaces where fuel is absent, which forces fire travel to pause. The recent popularity of gravel is ideal for expanding this "island" planting concept with mineral surfacing resistant to fire. Gravel roads, pathways, and open areas also contribute easy access to firefighters and their equipment and vehicles.

In the defensible space landscape there can be taller trees and shrubs, but they must be adequately separated so they do not present an unbroken avenue of fuel that allows fire to move quickly across the land. Avoid planting directly beneath these trees, not just to reduce competition for water but to prevent flames that can be wind driven into the flammable canopy.

Beach Washed Salmon Bay

Black Mexican Pebbles

Gold Tint Crushed (mined)

Pink Tint Crushed (mined)

Rainbow Cobbles

River Run Gray

Ground Plane Plant Selection Matrix

BOTANICAL NAME	COMMON NAME	ZONE	COLORS	TYPE
*Arctostaphylos**	Manzanita	3 and 7	Pink, white	Creeping shrub
Arctotis hybrids	African Daisy	9	Many	Herbaceous
Carpobrotus edulis	Iceplant	7	Many	Succulent
Ceanothus griseus var. *horizontalis**	Creeping California Lilac	8	Blue	Creeping shrub
Cephalophyllum speciosum	Red Spike Iceplant	10	Red	Succulent
Cistus 'Sunset'	Hybrid Rockrose	8	Magenta	Creeping shrub
Dalea greggii	Trailing Indigo Bush	10	Violet	Creeping shrub
Delosperma cooperi	Iceplant	8	Many	Succulent
Lampranthus spectabilis	Trailing Iceplant	9	Many	Succulent
Lantana montevidensis	Creeping Lantana	10	Many	Creeping shrub
Rosmarinus officinalis 'Prostratus'	Creeping Rosemary	8	Blue	Creeping shrub
Thymus serpyllum	Creeping Thyme	4	Pink	Herbaceous
Vinca major, Vinca minor	Common Periwinkle	7	Blue	Herbaceous

*Indicates California native species.

5 Eye-Catching Accents

For every plant lost to drought or climate change, opportunities arise to make your garden better than ever. It's so easy to be satisfied with the status quo, but when we are forced to make changes, the result can be unexpectedly rewarding. The key is realizing that every plant replaced becomes a design project that potentially revamps that spot altogether.

Why Use Accents?

A landscape that lacks accent plants tends to be uniform and short on visual interest. When there's a primary visual hierarchy of plants, this helps people intuitively organize the garden. Accent plants are near the top of the hierarchy because they draw the eye to spots where attention is needed or desired. An accent can also fill narrow views to long-range problem spots such as side yards.

Accents in Containers

Accents are ideal for large pots and urns in gardens too small or unsuited to inground planting. They also let you grow frost-tender plants you can move indoors for winter when potted. The big, burly containers suited to larger plants can indeed help save water when they are irrigated with a drip system. Watering this way eliminates excessive loss through the drainage hole in the typical potted plant, ensuring most of the moisture applied is absorbed by the potting soil. Simply install a battery-operated system timer to free you of watering chores.

Lighting the Accent Plant

Illuminating your accent creates a beating heart for the night garden. Depth is lost in the dark, but when a faraway accent is lighted, it adds instant depth to what was impenetrable darkness.

It's fun to experiment with lighting accent plants using high-intensity low-voltage lighting systems—just start lighting the accent plants, then the rest takes care of itself.

- If you put the light in front of the plant, you'll lose detail and some color because of glare.

- A wall or building behind that front-lighted plant becomes a shadow show.

- A backlight on a plant makes it stand dark in silhouette.

- An uplighted plant literally glows from the inside up.

Accent Plants

Key

Sun			Bloom Season				Region				
●	◐	○	✾	☀	⚜	❄	HD	LD	M	C	IV
SHADE	PARTLY SUNNY	SUN	SPRING	SUMMER	FALL	WINTER	HIGH DESERT	LOW DESERT	MOUN-TAINS	COAST	INLAND VALLEY

AGAVE

Agave americana (Blue Agave)

Height	Width	Zone	Sun	Bloom Season	Region	Flower Color
6'	8'	8	○	✾	LD	Bronze

America's favorite, the big blue agave, is a hallmark of California and the Southwest and is not only monumental in size, it is the most adaptable to a wide range of soils. This one can prove its worth in clay as well as sand. Large plants make a significant splash of cool blue year-round. The mother plant lives just 10 years before it flowers and dies, survived by the many offsets (baby plants) that grow around the base to sustain the colony. This is one of the most widely available succulents to buy, but large specimens transplant easily if rescued from other sites. This species is the most vulnerable to agave snout weevil and should be avoided in regions or gardens where this pest is present.

ALOE

Height	Width	Zone	Sun		Bloom Season	Region		Flower Color
6'–20'	Variable	9–10	◑	○	✿	LD	C	Red orange

Large upright aloes are among the most outstanding succulents for landscaping because of their size and longevity, but sensitivity to frost limits them to coastal Southern California and some inland tropical desert zones. Aloes that develop upright trunks are such slow growers it's worth the expense to purchase a large specimen for immediate results. These aloes share a thick rigid upright branching trunk topped with rosettes of broad spiny-edged leaves. All originate in southern Africa where they take heat and drought in stride. *Aloe marlothii* is harvested as a source of aloe gel sold often as that of *Aloe vera*. Where winter conditions are too cold, these big aloes make excellent container succulents that can be moved into a sunroom or greenhouse for the cold months. Where aloe is grown in ground, try protecting it with a Planket or bedsheet on unusually cold nights. (Plankets are lightweight plant covers from the garden center with handy shapes and drawstrings to make covering a lot easier.) Aloes take on bright red and orange coloring from both drought and cold, then all bloom in an explosion of hot-colored tubular flowers irresistible to hummingbirds. These three aloe species listed by their overall size are widely available from growers in mild winter regions:

Tree Aloes

Botanical Name	Common Name	Height	Zone
Aloe marlothii	Mountain Aloe	6'–8'	9
Aloe dichotoma	Quiver Tree	15'–20'	9–10
Aloe barberae or *A. bainesii*	Tree Aloe	50'	9

BEAUCARNEA

Beaucarnea recurvata **(Ponytail Palm)**

Height	Width	Zone	Sun		Bloom Season	Region		Flower Color
12'–25'	6'–10'	8	◐	○	✿	LD	C	Cream

The genus name *Beaucarnea* translates as "beautiful flesh," describing the oversized caudex at the base of its treelike trunk. This is where the succulent tissues are concentrated for water storage. The big, round base lends an exotic, almost supernatural, appearance to its overall form. They're sold as single foliage head or with multiples, each topped with its own tresses of linear foliage that sway with the slightest breeze. For modern gardens in need of just one great specimen to define an outdoor living space, this plant is positively amazing uplighted. *Beaucarnea* is not a big bloomer but is perfectly tailored to tall, wide pots that bring this caudex off the ground and raise the foliage head enough to provide a vertical accent. Move pots indoors for cooler winter zones because ponytail trees are proven houseplants as well.

BRUGMANSIA

Brugmansia suaveolens hybrids (Angel's Trumpet)

No other plant provides quite the same dramatic appeal as the angel's trumpet. The foot-long flowers are plentiful and evening fragrant to lure pollinating moths. Because of its origins in the woodlands of South America, angel's trumpet is the quintessential focal point for shady spaces. Though it's a frost-tender tropical, gardeners in cooler climates grow them outdoors in pots during the season, then move them to a frost-free area for winter deciduous storage. These beautiful plants are surprisingly common in West Coast beach towns with frost-free, maritime conditions. There is nothing more beautiful at short range than a beautifully pruned *Brugmansia* in full bloom. Large specimens and many cultivars can be found at quality garden centers.

> **WARNING:** Botanical Toxin
>
> As a member of the notorious Nightshade family, all parts of the angel's trumpet are poisonous to humans and pets. Toxins from leaves can enter the body through the skin, particularly in the heat when pores are wide open, so use gloves when handling this plant.

CAESALPINIA

Caesalpinia gilliesii (Bird-of-Paradise Bush)

Height	Width	Zone	Sun		Bloom Season		Region			Flower Color
8'	10'	7	◐	○	✿	☀	HD	LD	IV	Yellow

This South American beauty deserves a much larger presence in western gardens. Not only is it bright and exotic, plants are both tolerant of extreme drought and surprisingly cold hardy. Formerly known only in desert communities, these plants should be used more in inland valleys, but avoid cool night moisture of the immediate coast. It makes a fine single accent that doesn't suck the light out of a space or present a too-emerald shade of green. Nothing makes a better match for western natives or as a hummingbird draw. Use this plant as a transparent foreground accent.

Caesalpinia pulcherrima, called poinciana in the tropics, is a close relative unique to tropical low desert and throughout the Caribbean. This plant has little frost tolerance, so summer heat stimulates heavy bloom in fiery-orange/yellow clusters. This plant dies back to the ground each winter, where it remains unattractive until heat returns.

CERCIS

Cercis occidentalis (Western Redbud)

Height	Width	Zone	Sun	Bloom Season	Region			Flower Color	Type
20'	15'	7	O	✿	M	C	IV	Pink	Deciduous

Adapted to the long dry season of the western slope of the Sierra Nevada, this smaller redbud is far more drought resistant than its more popular cousin, *Cercis canadensis*. It's an ideal deciduous accent for seasonal change in gardens of suburban and rural homes. In very mild winters it may not flower as prolifically as it does where there's cold, and blossom density may depend on rainfall. The redbud has two seasons of outstanding color. It blooms very early before the foliage for bold color masses. Then, in the dry late summer around August, redbuds in the wild go dormant,

gradually changing leaf color to hazy whiskey sunset hues. Only if you cut back on irrigation by the end of August will garden redbuds show you this wild fall change. This is an excellent plant for two seasons of bold hues to blend with both exotics and western natives.

CHILOPSIS

Chilopsis linearis hybrids (Desert Willow)

Height	Width	Zone	Sun	Bloom Season			Region		Flower Color	Type
10'–20'	10'–15'	7	O	🎋	☀	🍁	HD	LD	Pink, red	Deciduous

Desert willow is a deciduous, open rangy native tree of the desert Southwest found often along the banks of dry washes and in canyons. The exquisite beauty of its unique flowers makes this a standout in the wild, but the species is too large a plant for a typical accent. These smaller named hybrids produce larger, more intensely colored flowers that rival that of orchids in beauty. Each of these varieties has its own unique dimensions, hardiness, and characteristics, such as 'Dark Storm' developed in Texas for that state's unique climatic conditions. The hybrids have not yet become as popular as they should be throughout the West, but drought will drive them into the market, making these formerly little-known plants some of the most outstanding solutions for drier landscapes.

Smaller *Chilopsis* Varieties for Accents

Variety	Flower Color	Height
'Bubba'	Pink	20'
'Burgundy'	Maroon	15'–20'
'Dark Storm'	Purple	15'–20'
'Art's Seedless'	Pink spotted	10'
'Lucretia Hamilton'	Reddish purple	15'
'Mesquite Valley Pink'	Dark pink	20'

Chilopsis linearis

Chilopsis 'Warren Jones'

Chilopsis 'Bubba'

Hybrid desert willow

CORDYLINE

Cordyline australis 'Burgundy Spire' (Grass Palm)

Height	Width	Zone	Sun	Bloom Season	Region		Flower Color
20'	8'	9	O	⊛	C	IV	White

These beautiful strap-leaf accent plants are closely related to *Dracaena* houseplants. The best accent *Cordyline* are those that produce trunks, some reaching 20 feet tall with age. In the landscape these big, bold foliage plants are as well suited to modern design or visually exotic gardens. These are easy plants to grow and stand up well to coastal winds, but they have difficulty with desiccation and die back in very hot, dry inland locales.

Cordyline australis Varieties with Purple Foliage

'Bauer's Dracaena'
'Burgundy Spire'
'Cabernet'
'Purple Sensation'
'Red Star'

FOUQUIERIA

Fouquieria splendens (Ocotillo)

Height	Width	Zone	Sun	Bloom Season	Region		Flower Color	Type
10'	8'	8	O	⚘	HD	LD	Red	Deciduous

Ocotillo has long been a staple of the desert landscape because of its bold upright form and ease of cultivation. Clusters of red tubular flowers in spring attract hummingbirds and carpenter bees. The plant is composed of a bundle of stiff rods that create a transparent plant, exceptional under night lighting. This native adapts to drought by shedding its leaves up to ten times per year. Those in Arizona are adapted to the summer monsoons where they flourish after cloudbursts. In low-desert landscapes the ocotillo shows its desire for both water and fertilizer, with some of the biggest specimens growing adjacent to well-fed lawns.

TIP: Old-school gardeners learned to spray the dormant leafless ocotillo plant with water in the heat of summer to stimulate the monsoon reaction that begins rapid leaf development.

PHORMIUM

Phormium tenax (New Zealand Flax)

Height	Width	Zone	Sun		Bloom Season	Region		Flower Color
3'–6'	3'–6'	8	◑	○	☼	C	IV	Bronze

Flax came into its own in the mid-twentieth century along the freeways of Southern California. The original species of stiff strap leaves matures at up to 10 feet tall, so it makes a very large accent plant that is even more wonderful when its exotic bronze flower spikes rise to bloom. However, this species can become a monster with time and may prove difficult in smaller spaces. Contemporary breeding in Australia has resulted in new flax varieties with dramatic colors from black to bright yellow. Powerfully colored flax hybrids are often smaller than the species and better adapted to pots and tight spaces.

New Zealand Flax Varieties for Bold Color Accents

Variety	Height	Color
'Atropurpureum'	5'–6'	Leathery purple red
'Black Adder'	3'–4'	Very dark bronze, black
'Golden Ray'	3'–4'	Olive green, creamy edges, pinkish tinge
'Pink Stripe'	4'–5'	Bronzy green with pink edges
'Rainbow Chief'	5'–6'	Pink with red highlights
'Rainbow Queen'	3'–4'	Bronzy with salmon-striped edges
'Sundowner'	5'	Bronze green, edges and stripes in coral red

YUCCA

Height	Width	Zone	Sun	Bloom Season	Region		Flower Color
15'	3'–6'	6	O	✿	HD	LD	White

Some *Yucca* species are ground-dwelling foliage rosettes and others develop tree-height trunks. When you're using yucca as an accent plant, choose those that develop trunks because they offer height and interest and make superior specimens for night lighting. *Yucca* flowers are carried on tall stalks that rise above the foliage so that moth pollinators can reach them in the dark. Blooms are always white to reflect moonlight and starlight to draw moths. This has long made yucca a part of moon garden compositions that light up under natural lunar glow, and in the West they are a big part of pollinator-oriented desert landscapes. Because of the yucca's slow growth, it's recommended that focal-point yuccas be obtained from large container-grown specimens so they offer plenty of color and height and bloom reliably from day one.

Botanical Name	Common Name	Zone	Height
Yucca elata	Soaptree Yucca	6	15'
Yucca gloriosa	Spanish Dagger	6	16'
Yucca rostrata	Beaked Yucca	7	16'

Accents for Austere Modern Gardens

The austerity of landscapes for modern architecture depends heavily on accents. Because modern design lacks decoration, it is generally placid and visually quiet because of overall simplicity. The accent plant can become the most important part of the landscape picture. The late Brazilian landscape architect Roberto Burle Marx created large city plantings using nothing but ground plane materials, spreading plants and carefully selected upstanding accents to create groundbreaking modern landscapes.

FIVE-PLANT PALETTE: MODERN

1. *Agave americana* (Blue Agave)

2. *Beaucarnea recurvata* (Ponytail Palm)

3. *Chondropetalum tectorum* (Cape Rush)

4. *Dasylirion longissimum* (Mexican Grass Tree)

5. *Echinocactus grusonii* (Golden Barrel)

Accents with Perennial Foliage Color

With many new species and varieties of plants, the most useful are those with perpetually colorful foliage. Designers realize that these colored-leaf plants offer year-round beauty. The problem with flowering accents is how they look when not flowering, which is why plants with variegated foliage, bronze hues, stripes, and other characteristics are in high demand. They are also low maintenance and lack the litter associated with spent reproductive structures.

Five-Plant Palette: Foliage Color

BOTANICAL NAME	COMMON NAME	COLOR
Agave americana	Blue Agave	Blue gray
Aloe marlothii	Mountain Aloe	Red, orange, green
Cercis occidentalis	Western Redbud	Fall foliage—smoky sunset colors
Cordyline australis 'Burgundy Spire'	Grass Palm	Bronze and burgundy
Phormium tenax hybrids	New Zealand Flax	Yellow, bronze, black, coral, pink

Accent Plant Flower Color Selection Guide by Genus

	PURPLE	PINK	WHITE	YELLOW	RED	ORANGE
Aloe				✓	✓	✓
Beaucarnea			✓	✓		
Caesalpinia				✓	✓	✓
Cercis		✓				
Chilopsis		✓	✓		✓	
Fouquieria					✓	
Yucca			✓	✓		

Accent Plant Selection Matrix

BOTANICAL NAME	COMMON NAME	ZONE	COLORS	TYPE
Agave americana	Blue Agave	8	Bronze	Succulent
Aloe marlothii	Mountain Aloe	9	Red orange	Succulent
Aloe barberae	Tree Aloe	9	Orange red	Succulent
Aloe dichotoma	Quiver Tree	9–10	Yellow	Succulent
Beaucarnea recurvata	Ponytail Palm	8	Cream	Succulent
Brugmansia suaveolens	Angel's Trumpet	10	White, yellow, pink	Tropical
Caesalpinia gilliesii	Bird-of-Paradise Bush	7	Yellow	Desert
Caesalpinia pulcherrima	Poinciana	9–10	Red orange, yellow	Tropical
Cercis occidentalis	Western Redbud	7	Pink	Tree
Chilopsis linearis hybrids	Desert Willow	7	Pink, purple, burgundy, red, white	Tree
Cordyline australis 'Burgundy Spire'	Grass Palm	9	White	Tropical
Fouquieria splendens	Ocotillo	8	Red	Succulent
Phormium tenax	New Zealand Flax	8	Bronze	Tropical
Yucca elata	Soaptree Yucca	6	White	Succulent
Yucca gloriosa	Spanish Dagger	6	White	Succulent
Yucca rostrata	Beaked Yucca	7	White	Succulent

*Indicates California native species.

Ephemeral Flowers for Seasonal Color

The word *ephemeral* defines anything that lives for just a short time. It's often used to define flowering plants that are annuals, which grow from seed, mature, flower, and set new seed within just a single growing season. Those suited for dry gardens can be divided into three loosely defined categories:

Annual wildflowers are by far the best example of ephemeral plants yet are among the most misunderstood and underappreciated garden plants for drought. Do not confuse these with perennial wildflowers, which are slower to germinate and more difficult to establish from seed.

....

Tender bedding plants cannot survive a frost, so they're absolutely limited to growing season and will be cut down by the first cold mornings of fall. These may be annuals or very fast-growing perennials from mild winter regions that offer lots of color for limited amounts of water.

....

Bulbs and their kin are a third group of ephemeral plants with growth strictly limited to the rainy season. For example, daffodils originate in arid North Africa and the western Mediterranean where their growing season is typically during the cool, moist winter months, so they come and go before the heat and low humidity of summer. This unusual season of growth is a drought adaptation from their habitat of origin that allows them to lie underground, dormant without a drop of water from about June until early winter.

....

Wildflowers

Even though there is little rain during drought, it does return in the end. Where we're conserving water seasonal rains still come, however brief. If the desert in all its austerity can put on such a show, then the wildflower is indeed the queen of all dry gardens. She needs no water from us to bloom her heart out.

The American West is home to a huge range of wildflowers that come and go during their brief show in spring. California poppy and Texas bluebonnet are among quintessential spring flowers of this rugged country that make fine spring color for dry gardens without asking for much or any irrigation. Many of these species are adapted to very poor soils, cliff faces, and rocky ground where they experience less competition than they would in fertile grassy lowlands.

SEVEN REASONS WILDFLOWER SOWINGS FAIL

1. **Old seed.** Always buy new seed each year and store it in a cool, dry place until you're ready to sow. Some species have a limited period of viability and may not survive more than a year in storage.

2. **Wrong seed.** Failure to plant wildflowers adapted to your local climate can cause widespread failure of germination, stunted seedlings, disease, and pest attacks. Strive to grow several local native wildflowers to ensure they are well adapted, and only then experiment with new options so you don't risk the whole stand.

3. **Seed covered too deeply.** Don't cover this seed; just lightly rake it into soft ground for optimal coverage and quick germination.

4. **Soil too rich.** Many wildflowers prefer porous, well-drained soils. This is why they are found on sloping ground, often on south-facing inclines. Small annual lupine often grows densely along road edges where they root into the base gravel. This reduces competition from needier plants and allows runoff to quickly penetrate to feed fast-growing roots.

5. **Competing plants.** Some wildflowers cannot survive competition. It's usually caused by more demanding plants like greedy grasses and aggressive exotic weeds that shade the flowers and invade their root zone. It's important to control weeds the season before to reduce competition before sowing. Failing to do so means you'll have to handpick the weeds, if you can spot them among the desirable seedlings that may appear identical to the untrained eye.

6. **Seeds sown too late.** Sowing wildflowers in the late fall just before the rainy season begins is crucial to those species that germinate in winter and develop larger root systems for adaptation to hot, dry climates.

7. **Wildlife.** Birds, rabbits, and many other forms of wildlife love your seed, and unless properly covered or protected with mulch or fencing, it may be gobbled up during the lean months. This is the biggest drawback to sowing too early.

GREAT DIGS FOR WILDFLOWERS

In the early spring when dry streambeds sprout their load of early wildflowers, it's like a miracle at winter's end. These otherwise parched places are often the only ones sandy-gravelly enough for many wildflower species to flourish. Older gravel fields and rock gardens of succulents often explode into bloom as well. Again, the soil should be well drained and conditions sunny. The third option is gentle slopes or steeper ones that include boulders or walls or terraces where drainage is assured. These are the sites where some types are likely to do well, and, if happy enough, they self-sow for next year. However, it's rare to have a second season as good as the first, because the species not willing to reproduce there die out, leaving the more successful ones to naturalize.

THEY LIKE IT DISTURBED

Red corn poppies (*Papaver rhoeas*), a wildflower of Europe, grow in wheat fields because they love to germinate in disturbed soils. In France, trench warfare of World War I fertilized poppies with the blood of thousands, resulting in an epic crop of poppies after the armistice. This demonstrates that poppies and many other wildflowers prefer to be sowed into scarred, plowed, ripped, or newly cleared ground, where they germinate easily compared to packed established earth. Seeds thrown onto irregular ground filter down into the nooks and crannies where rain quickly covers them with a thin layer of soil. Moisture also remains in these pockets to keep seedlings adequately hydrated in open ground.

TIP: Whenever you disturb a lot of ground, from grading a homesite to the first tilling of a new backyard, sow wildflowers for beauty and erosion control. Get the kids involved with broadcasting seed. When the rains come they will be excited when it all explodes into bloom. Sowing wildflowers doesn't just result in beautiful flowers; it helps provide soil coverage, erosion control, and a huge buffet of nectar for local insects and hummingbirds.

SEEDS OF CHANGE

A number of excellent American seed houses sell wildflower seed online or via mail order, so you can peruse the various mixes to find the one best suited for your homesite. Wildflower seed is sold by packet or weight, so you can buy in bulk. Seed stock is divided into individual species or seed mixes that are blended for different climates and outcomes. The great benefit of a mix for first-time users is the ability to discover which wildflowers do best in your yard. Once you know which germinate readily and reach maturity to bloom well, you can sow more of these seeds in the future with confidence they will thrive. Here are how seed mixes differ and why:

Seed blends: These mixes include the most widely adapted species found in most states.

....

Native blends: These wildflowers are selected by their local nativity and feature many species unique or endemic to certain areas.

....

Regional blends: Regional mixes suit a wide climatic range with natives, exotic species, and some new varieties to offer the widest range of plant forms and flower colors.

....

Climatic blends: A climate area such as the Pacific Northwest can have its own tailored seed mixes that are perfectly adapted to high rainfall, cloudy conditions, and cooler temperatures.

....

Wildflowers

Key

Sun			Bloom Season				Region				
●	◐	○	✿	☼	⚜	❄	HD	LD	M	C	IV
SHADE	PARTLY SUNNY	SUN	SPRING	SUMMER	FALL	WINTER	HIGH DESERT	LOW DESERT	MOUN-TAINS	COAST	INLAND VALLEY

BAILEYA MULTIRADIATA (DESERT MARIGOLD)

Height	Width	Zone	Sun	Bloom Season	Region				Flower Color
12"	18"	6	○	✿	HD	LD	M	IV	Yellow

This great wild-looking plant lives for about 2 years, eagerly reseeding itself into sandy-gravelly ground in the desert. A beautiful tuft of gray foliage topped with golden daisies, it spreads by underground rhizomes if fully naturalized. This is the quintessential choice for dry streambeds and gravel gardens, where its open rangy character looks best standing alone or in small groups as it would in nature. Otherwise it is too easily lost amid greener, more lush plants. Take advantage of its transparent nature and blend into very dry spaces with cacti to provide more visual interest without additional moisture. Plants naturally die back late in the summer but under limited irrigation they may bloom far longer. This is a great choice for all desert scenarios, dry mountains where soils are decomposed granite, and on slopes and embankments. Plant from quarts or from seed.

COREOPSIS TINCTORIA (GOLDEN TICKSEED)

Height	Width	Zone	Sun	Bloom Season	Region					Flower Color
18"	2'–4'	2	O	✿	HD	LD	M	C	IV	Yellow

This tall flower bearing showy yellow-and-brown daises is commonly found west of the Rockies over a very large range, but also farther east. This is the *Coreopsis* common in most western wildflower mixes, proving its widespread adaptability. It's a biennial with a 2-year life span that prefers sandy soils with limited fertility. It does very well in open spaces and as an erosion control plant. After flowers fade you can deadhead them for a more tidy plant or allow them to go to seed and self-sow for next year. Hardy to Zone 2, this seed is quite capable of wintering over in the soil of northern states and high mountain gardens with significant cold. Like most wildflowers it will not abide heavy clays or saturated ground.

DATURA METELOIDES (JIMSON WEED)

Height	Width	Zone	Sun		Bloom Season			Region					Flower Color
3'	4'	5	◐	○	❀	☼	⚜	HD	LD	M	C	IV	White

This large North American native is often seen along western roadsides in full bloom. It's a very large herbaceous plant that bears foot-long snow-white trumpet-shaped blooms that are at their best in the early morning hours. This is a night-pollinated species preferred by very large hawk or hummingbird moths drawn by the scent of the flowers, which stand out in bold contrast against dark forest-green foliage. Use *Datura* to add darker green foliage where gray and blue green predominate in the dry garden. A lover of rocky infertile ground, *Datura* thrives where other plants fail. It's a natural among cacti and desert plants, but it is amazingly elegant for open spaces in spartan modern landscapes or as part of a floriferous dryland cottage garden. Grow from seed gathered from local plants or purchase seed from catalogs.

WARNING: Poisonous Alkaloids

All parts of *Datura* plants and flowers contain potent alkaloids that are poisonous. Do not plant where children and pets are present. Wear gloves when handling plants or pruning to ensure the poison does not enter through tiny cuts or is absorbed transdermally, particularly on hot days.

ESCHSCHOLZIA CALIFORNICA (CALIFORNIA POPPY)

Height	Width	Zone	Sun	Bloom Season	Region					Flower Color
6"–15"	6"–15"	5	○	❀	HD	LD	M	C	IV	Yellow orange

While treated as an annual wildflower, this native is actually a short-lived perennial that, once established, regrows each spring from the roots for a few years running. Unlike other natives, this poppy is not picky about soils so long as they are well drained. This poppy should be sown in gardens or in wildland settings in the fall so seed is exposed to the entire winter rainy season. Seeds germinate with the earliest rains to begin the taproot, key

to heat and drought tolerance. There is no better plant for adding to gaps in flagstone patios, gravel gardens, and transition zones between gardens and natural vegetation.

LUPINUS SUCCULENTUS (ARROYO LUPINE)

Height	Width	Zone	Sun	Bloom Season	Region					Flower Color
2'–3'	2'–3'	8	O	✿	HD	LD	M	C	IV	Blue

With many different species of wild lupine native to California, this annual is the largest overall. It is routinely grown from seed sown in the fall to create a large stand of color germinated by natural rainfall. Unlike other lupine that are particular about soil type and extreme drainage, this species takes dense soil and relatively level ground in stride. Seed for this plant is widely available from wildflower seed houses as individuals or as part of western wildflower mixes. Sow lupine to fill open spaces, disturbed ground, transitions to wildland and open space, rocky slopes and outcrops, and everywhere else there is full sun.

1. *Baileya multiradiata* (Desert Marigold)

2. *Datura meteloides* (Jimson Weed)

3. *Eschscholzia californica* (California Poppy)

4. *Gaura lindheimeri* (Gaura)

5. *Muhlenbergia rigens* (Deergrass)

EPHEMERAL FLOWERS FOR SEASONAL COLOR

Tender Bedding Plants

CUPHEA LLAVEA (BAT FACE CUPHEA)

Height	Width	Zone	Sun		Bloom Season	Region					Flower Color
18"	2'–3'	9	◐	○	☀	HD	LD	M	C	IV	Red, navy blue

This beautiful little herbaceous plant from Mexico is grown as an annual in the Southwest because it is quite frost tender. When planted from a quart-sized seedling, it quickly forms a rangy little 2- to 3-foot mound bearing the most unique flowers, each about the size of a quarter. The arrangement of magenta and navy-blue petals clearly resembles the face of a bat. A sun lover on the coast, this plant prefers afternoon shade inland and in the desert while maintaining low water conditions, which stimulate repeat blooming all summer long. This tender tropical will easily self-sow into sandy ground where it thrives in the rapid drainage. Flowers of volunteers will not match the color of the parent. This is an underappreciated yet highly charming candidate for cottage gardens, pots and troughs, or partially shaded sites inland around tree canopies or beneath larger specimen succulents.

LANTANA CAMARA HYBRIDS

Height	Width	Zone	Sun	Bloom Season				Region		Flower Color
2'–5'	3'–5'	9	O	✿	☀	🍁	❄	LD	C	Varies

Lantana is perennial in the tropics, such as Florida and other similar frost-free climates, where it is an invasive exotic. The seeds, inside berries attractive to birds, are carried far and wide beyond the garden to spread like weeds. For this reason breeders have sought to create new hybrids that are fruitless and sterile so there is little chance they can invade local wildlands or the rest of your garden. *Lantana* has mild frost resistance, but in most areas outside frost-free zones it's grown as a summer annual for difficult hot spots. With few demands, *Lantana* is our best source of seasonal color to spot into arid gardens or pots for the hot summer months.

Recommended Sterile *Lantana* Hybrids

Variety	Flower Color	Height
'Miss Huff'	Orange, gold	5'
'Mozelle'	Yellow, pink	5'
'New Gold'	Yellow	2'
'Patriot Deen Day Smith'	Pink, yellow, apricot	5'
'Patriot Marc Cathey'	White	5'
'Samantha'	Yellow	2'-3'

PORTULACA GRANDIFLORA (MOSS ROSE)

Height	Width	Zone	Sun	Bloom Season	Region	Flower Color
6"	12"	9	◑	✽	C	Many

This annual flower is a true succulent that hails from the dry, rocky soils of Brazil, Uruguay, and Argentina. Breeders have developed many different flower colors for these low-growing annuals that can be used as seasonal groundcovers. They are great for adding a huge range of intense flower colors to small rock gardens or cottage garden compositions. Where root-knot nematodes plague sandy soils, grow this flower in well-drained containers. Insert seedlings from six-packs into gaps in mixed succulent container gardens that often lack late summer color. Their spreading habit also makes them graceful as they dangle over edges and down slopes or serve as spot interest in dry flagstone gaps.

RUSSELIA EQUISETIFORMIS (FIRECRACKER PLANT)

Height	Width	Zone	Sun		Bloom Season			Region		Flower Color
3'–4'	3'–4'	9	◑	○	✿	☀	✾	LD	C	Red orange

This beautiful specimen native to Mexico is one of the most fabulous plants for standout foliage and flowers on a patio or garden. Thin, fine-textured foliage is almost hairlike as it cascades down the sides of pots. It's popular to grow in taller containers where it can flow off the edges. Its red tubular flowers are highly attractive to hummingbirds. This is a chameleon suited to tropical, Spanish, and modern landscape styles, depending on where and how it's used in ground or in a great pot.

SENECIO CINERARIA (DUSTY MILLER)

Height	Width	Zone	Sun		Bloom Season	Region			Flower Color
18"	18"	9	◑	○	✿	LD	C	IV	Yellow

Dusty miller has been a popular annual in American gardens for well over a century. It's beloved for bold silver foliage and golden daisies that give variety to annual flower compositions in ground and in containers. Gardeners have long cut off the developing flowers to stimulate larger and lusher foliage growth. It is yet another plant from the arid rocky bluffs of the Mediterranean and a great companion for rockroses and lavenders. It is very fast-growing and will reach 3 feet in a single season. Spot these plants in among your salvias and other heavy bloomers that lack volume to increase overall mass. Buy dusty miller in six-packs and plant early in the season to allow the longest possible growing time before frost arrives.

TRADESCANTIA PALLIDA (PURPLE TRADESCANTIA)

Height	Width	Zone	Sun		Bloom Season	Region		Flower Color
12"	18"	10	◑	○	☼	LD	C	Pink

Most know this as a houseplant, but it is a tropical heat lover that is suddenly popular for adding potent seasonal color to outdoor gardens. It's surprising to discover this former houseplant is a vigorous contender in the frost-free low desert or on the coast where it's amazingly tolerant of sun, high heat, and shade. It's a perfect fit for overflowing succulent pot edges into a purple cascade. It is fast-growing from nursery seedlings, or you can start your own from cuttings like any houseplant, so that you have plenty to fill out planting areas for pennies.

Bulbs

Fall-planted bulbs bring spring color to drought-stricken gardens because they demand little to no irrigation water to bloom, so you can put them anywhere in the sun where soils are well drained. Once planted in the warm autumn soil, plants become established naturally over winter. After they flower in the spring, only a small amount of water is required to feed the foliage until it naturally dies back before summer.

GRAVEYARD DAFFODILS

Throughout the inland West you will find daffodils blooming in old graveyards every spring. They have naturalized for two reasons. First these familiar bulbs contain toxins that prevent them from being gobbled by gophers. Secondly they originated in Asia Minor, that very cold, dry region that includes parts of the Middle East, from Turkey eastward to Asia. Daffodils are perfectly adapted to dry gardens because they grow during the wet winter and spring, then turn dormant for the rainless summer and fall. Add them to your droughty garden knowing they'll come and go all by themselves each year to come.

SOUTH AFRICAN BULBS

An example of the incredible flora of dry South Africa is found in the veldt, a prairie-like grassland that is blended with a wide range of flowering plants and succulents. Among them are two old-fashioned bulbs that are still sold with traditional spring bulbs after losing favor. Now they're being rediscovered as candidates for droughty gardens. Both *Ixia* and *Sparaxis* are endemic species of the Iris family found in these habitats where they thrive in full sun under coastal influence. Farther inland they prefer locations protected from hot afternoon exposure. These beautiful summer bloomers are corms ideal for rocky ground because they are planted just 2 inches deep and prefer to remain in place long term without digging or dividing. They are ideal for former lawn spaces now treated as mixed prairie plantings, or you can blend them in with native perennials into rock gardens and dry streambeds where they offer wildflower-delicate beauty for much of the summer.

IRIS GERMANICA (BEARDED IRIS)

Height	Width	Zone	Sun		Bloom Season		Region		Flower Color
2'–3'	12"–18"	6	◑	○	✿	☼	C	IV	Varies

Bearded iris is technically a summer bulb rarely listed as a drought-resistant plant, but it is well adapted for an arid seasonal show. If left to its own devices it thrives during the rainy season in the West, then becomes dormant for the summer after blooming. In fact, if grown as a droughty seasonal bloomer it actually does better than under irrigation because there's less moisture to cause the typical diseases that afflict its tuberous roots. Flowers occur on new rhizome growth. With hundreds of ordinary and super-fancy hybrids, there may be great variability in degree of drought tolerance from one variety to the next. More basic bearded iris flowers tend to be less finicky than the showy ones.

IXIA VIRIDIFLORA (WAND FLOWER)

Height	Width	Zone	Sun		Bloom Season	Region			Flower Color
12"–24"	6"–12"	10	◑	○	✿	LD	C	IV	Many

This distinctive red-and-yellow–flowered South African bulb originates in the Cape region where it adapts to persistent coastal winds by developing strong stems. Though it's only marginally frost hardy, the corms can be protected underground with mulch to grow in colder zones. This is a popular potted bulb that can be brought out while blooming, then set aside for the rest of the year. These are outstanding corms to blend into large native grasslands where they'll come and go with the seasons just as they do on the African veldt. However, its small, delicate size fits perfectly into urban yards, patios, and roof gardens.

SPARAXIS TRICOLOR (HARLEQUIN FLOWER)

Height	Width	Zone	Sun		Bloom Season	Region			Flower Color
4"–16"	8"	9	◑	○	✿	LD	C	IV	Many

Few bulbs feature such brilliantly colored blossoms as these easy-to-grow, heat-loving tender bulbs. Treat them as annuals where there's frost by planting with the spring rains. Just insert the inch-diameter hard corms 2 inches deep into the mud with a finger. The delicate plants look best when planted in groups to intensify visibility. They are often grouped in pots for an easy move to storage during colder winters. They're reliably perennial in frost-free coastal conditions but may require a bit of protection where it's colder inland.

Ephemeral Plant Selection Matrix

BOTANICAL NAME	COMMON NAME	TYPE	FLOWER COLOR	GROUP
*Baileya multiradiata**	Desert Marigold	Biennial	Yellow	Wildflower
*Coreopsis tinctoria**	Golden Tickseed	Biennial	Yellow	Wildflower
Cuphea llavea	Bat Face Cuphaea	Annual	Red, blue	Bedding/ pots
*Datura meteloides**	Jimson Weed	Perennial	White	Wildflower
*Eschscholzia californica**	California Poppy	Annual	Gold	Wildflower
Iris germanica	Bearded Iris	Rhizome	Many	Bulbs
Ixia viridiflora	Wand Flower	Corm	Many	Bulbs
Lantana camara hybrids	Hybrid Lantana	Perennial	Varies	Bedding/ pots
*Lupinus succulentus**	Arroyo Lupine	Annual	Blue	Wildflower
Narcissus hybrids	Daffodil	Spring bulb	White, yellow	Bulbs
Portulaca grandiflora	Moss Rose	Annual	Many	Bedding/ pots
Russelia equisetiformis	Firecracker Plant	Perennial	Red orange	Bedding/ pots
Senecio cineraria	Dusty Miller	Annual	Yellow	Bedding/ pots
Sparaxis tricolor	Harlequin Flower	Corm	Many	Bulbs
Tradescantia pallida	Purple Tradescantia	Perennial	Pink	Bedding/ pots

*Indicates California native species.

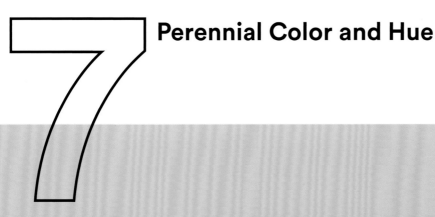

Perennial Color and Hue

This chapter celebrates perennial plants that flower heavily each year without extra water or care for the dry residential garden in inhospitable locations. They're selected for ease of cultivation. This is the cottage garden palette in all its glory, pared down to the most reliable and showy individuals for drought-resistant landscapes. These are not just western states natives but the best introductions from dry places around the world, such as Russian sage, South African red hot poker, and lavenders from southern Europe.

What Is a Perennial?

A perennial lives for many years versus an annual that grows from scratch each spring and dies with the frost. Perennials must be locally cold hardy to survive the winter. These are your most fabulous low-maintenance bloomers that grow larger and larger over time so the floral show is always expanding. The fully herbaceous plants often spread into many growth points that can be divided in the off-season into a bunch of new plants to spread around the garden economically. Every perennial you plant may become the genesis of your favorite part of the garden one day as you mix and match form and color into a stunning composition.

Arid Zone Perennials in the Landscape

Before you install any new plant, it's important to understand the role of each perennial in the overall landscape and ways it contributes visual characteristics to a site.

Replacement: Try compositions as a replacement rather than a one-for-one exchange. A large plant lost to drought can be replaced by a group of smaller perennials carefully chosen to fill its former growing space. Compose the group just as you would compose a painting, carefully blending color, texture, and form for a distinctive look.

....

Tiers or Layering: Understanding the mature height of your perennials is vital to their place in the planter and overall visibility. Taller plants like matilija poppy with its bushy growth habit belong in the rear of the space, with shorter plants stepping down in front. This not only ensures you get a good look at each plant but also that they won't block each other's light.

....

Color Strategy: Blend new plant colors into the existing garden color palette for more interest and diversity. Hot-colored flowers combine to provide a busy, active feel. Cool-colored flowers offer a gentle, refreshing effect. Mix and match these "color temperatures" to solve problems, add contrast, and emphasize depth.

Slopes: Perennials can turn a barren slope into a beautiful garden, particularly when there are rocks and boulders to give it interest and create nooks and crannies for the plants to thrive. Western natives often prefer sloping ground where drainage is assured. The same is true of Mediterranean species adapted to coastal palisades where they thrive in the maritime climate.

TIP: A plant's mature diameter tells you how much area it needs, while the plant's height tells how far back in the border it belongs.

PERENNIAL COLOR AND HUE

How to Plant on Slopes

The big problem with slopes is that water runs off before soils or plants have time to take it up. Therefore landscapers have developed a basic planting method that provides a pocket above the plant to catch runoff, holding it until it seeps down into the root ball. The spoils dug to make that pocket are mounded on the downhill side to create a berm that holds surface water directly over the root ball. This combination of two water-holding basins helps retain rainwater for more on-site utilization.

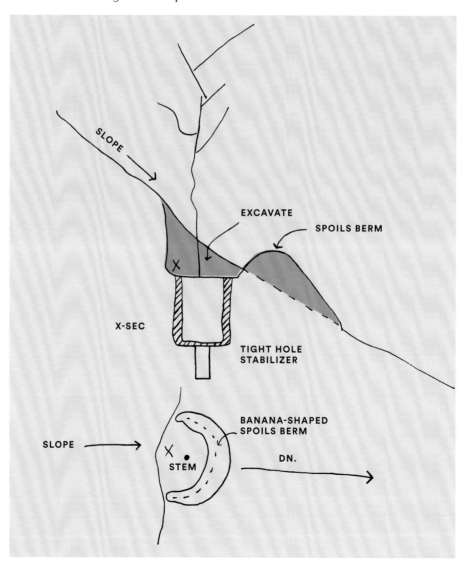

Perennials for Dry Gardens

Key

Sun			Bloom Season				Region				
●	◑	○	✿	☀	🍂	❄	HD	LD	M	C	IV
SHADE	PARTLY SUNNY	SUN	SPRING	SUMMER	FALL	WINTER	HIGH DESERT	LOW DESERT	MOUN-TAINS	COAST	INLAND VALLEY

ACHILLEA

Achillea millefolium (Yarrow)

Height	Width	Zone	Sun		Bloom Season		Region				Flower Color
2'	1'–2'	3	◑	○	✿	☀	HD	M	C	IV	Yellow, varies

The European herb called yarrow was carried by Romans wherever their armies traveled because it is a natural blood coagulant. Today we recognize it as a Mediterranean perennial tolerant of long, hot, dry seasons. It's perfectly sized for rock gardens as well as highbrow formal borders. The species may spread by underground rhizomes into a sizable mass if not divided. Fine aromatic "million leaf" foliage offers a soft, fuzzy clump bearing stiff, upright flower stalks topped

with dense clusters of small flowers. These are "everlastings," a popular dried flower. Hybrids are available in many hues to bring color to your garden with this single drought-resistant, surprisingly cold-hardy species.

Achillea 'Coronation Gold'

Achillea 'Richard Nelson'

Achillea 'Red Velvet'

CONVOLVULUS

Convolvulus cneorum (Bush Morning Glory, Silverbush)

Height	Width	Zone	Sun		Bloom Season	Region			Flower Color
2'–4'	2'–4'	8	◑	○	✿	LD	C	IV	White

You'll find *Convolvulus cneorum* on exposed limestone bluffs of the Mediterranean Sea from Spain to Albania, proving tolerance of exposed coastal conditions and a very long dry season. In the summer furnace of the low desert, it has exceptional tolerance of heat and lean soils. It is highly tolerant of alkaline soils and hard water common in the Southwest. The lovely white flowers shaped like that of the traditional morning glory vine are plentiful on dense mounds of olive-green leaves with a shiny silvery backing. This perennial lends a unique appearance under moonlight. Its preference for rocky fissures allows it to thrive where most don't as an exceptional slope plant.

DIETES

Dietes vegeta a.k.a. Moraea iridioides (Fortnight Lily)

Height	Width	Zone	Sun		Bloom Season		Region		Flower Color
3'–4'	3'–4'	8	◑	○	✽	☼	C	IV	White

Fortnight lily is among the most common plants in California gardens because it seems to always be in bloom. With beautiful white iris flowers atop dark green, narrow sword leaves, this southern African native is the ideal choice for the dry garden. It adds interest to dry streambeds to suggest water iris or reeds. This is a tough and vigorous plant that thrives in ordinary soils under minimal water. Very large clumps with age produce huge flower crops. A sibling of this species, *Dietes bicolor*, produces smaller, more rounded flowers in a pale iridescent yellow. This creamy species makes a more exotic-looking bloom for tropical looks; the white-flowered species better resembles a traditional iris.

ENCELIA

Encelia farinosa (Brittlebush, Incienso)

Height	Width	Zone	Sun	Bloom Season	Region		Flower Color
2'–3'	2'–3'	8	O	⚛	HD	LD	Golden yellow

Brittlebush is among the most common native perennials of southeastern California's blistering low desert with its granular, infertile soils. In gardens with a small amount of water this weather-efficient native becomes a big floriferous plant that grows fast and asks for little to no care. Silvery leaves help reflect high UV rates to increase drought resistance. The whole plant is topped with bright golden daisies on wiry stems in spring. Use where high temperatures and persistent drying winds are tough on less adapted species. Although it is hardy only to Zone 8 or about 20 degrees F, the roots will survive to recover after just 15 degrees F or even less. Brittlebush is perfect for larger landscapes for long-range seasonal interest or where browsing wildlife prevents other plants. Overwatering truncates its life span.

EUPHORBIA

Euphorbia rigida (Gopher Plant)

Height	Width	Zone	Sun	Bloom Season	Region			Flower Color
2'	3'	7	⭕	✿	HD	LD	C	Yellow

Although it looks like a tender perennial, this tough-as-nails plant is common in blistering low-desert gardens as well as moist coastal communities. Tolerant of poor but well-drained soils, it thrives where others fail because this is a succulent perennial. Because of its toxic white sap, gophers will not disturb this species of *Euphorbia* or its relatives, which makes this an important problem solver where any kind of rodent is an issue. It originates around the Mediterranean and in colder Asia Minor where it tolerates both extreme heat and considerable cold. Lovely blue-green foliage is topped with clusters of small, bright lemon-yellow flowers.

WARNING: White Euphorbia Sap

Often confused with cacti, these are succulents that bleed white latex sap if you injure them. The latex contains potent phytotoxins that can blister skin, burn eyes, and elicit allergic reactions. When you're growing any kind of *Euphorbia* in the dry garden, be careful when transplanting and pruning, particularly when children and pets are present.

GAURA

Gaura lindheimeri (Gaura)

Height	Width	Zone	Sun		Bloom Season		Region					Flower Color
3'–4'	4'–5'	5	◑	○	✿	☀	⚜	HD	LD	M	C	IV	White, pink

This perennial from the wilds of Texas and northern Mexico has proven to be one of the finest drought-resistant perennials. Open, light, and bright with an overall fine texture, it is highly successful in desert and all dry gardens. This is a taprooted plant, which is perfectly tailored to single-point delivery of drip irrigation for a super-efficient utilization of every drop. Long, thin wands bear lovely, delicate quarter-sized flowers, which continue to bloom over a very long season. A number of excellent hybrids vary flower color in shades of pink or white, and they offer smaller sizes better suited to limited spaces. This is a fine perennial for dry perennial borders, for visual relief from coarse-textured succulents, and for adding charm to cottage garden compositions.

KNIPHOFIA

Kniphofia uvaria (Red Hot Poker, Torch Lily)

Height	Width	Zone	Sun	Bloom Season	Region		Flower Color
2'–3'	2'–3'	7	O	⚘	C	IV	Red orange

Hardy and resilient, the torch lily has great stalked flowers that are a bright and festive addition to any garden style. A native of South Africa, this species is composed of a clump of blue-green sword-shaped leaves often found in the veldt grasslands. The flowers are tubular, much like the aloes in color and shape, so hummingbirds can't resist them. Unlike so many other arid zone natives, this species is far more tolerant of dense soils with more average drainage for greater adaptability. The thick, succulent root system can survive total loss of foliage to fire, drought, and cold, allowing it to be grown in colder areas if the roots are protected in winter. Hybrids offer diverse flower coloring and scaled-down varieties for urban conditions. Grown in western gardens for a century, this plant has proven itself and deserves far greater attention for water conservation.

LAVANDULA

Height	Width	Zone	Sun	Bloom Season	Region					Flower Color
2'–5'	2'–5'	5–8	○	✿	HD	LD	M	C	IV	Blue

Everyone loves lavender for its luscious scent and intense blue or purple flowers. Drought is the perfect opportunity to plant them all around your garden where water-loving perennials once lived. These plants are technically subshrubs with a moisture-sensitive root crown where they will rot if conditions are too wet. Where soils are heavy, growers plant their lavenders on raised rows to ensure the crowns stay high and dry during winter rains. Because of its

origins in mild southern Europe, growers have sought to increase tolerance of moisture and winter cold to allow commercial cultivation farther north. As a result there are literally hundreds of different forms with unique flowers, colors, and foliage, with new ones introduced every year. There are three basic species that figure largely into western gardens, each with slightly different hardiness. Within each species are many named varieties offering a huge range of choices for dry gardens.

Lavandula angustifolia
(English Lavender)

This species of northern Spain is the genesis of the English garden varieties because of its adaptation to colder winters, but it is not as drought or heat tolerant as *L. stoechas* or *L. dentata*. Slender violet flowers rise taller than any other species, up to 3 feet for a truly striking plant.

Lavandula dentata (French Lavender)

Very drought resistant, the dense gray corrugated foliage and medium-sized medium-blue flowers are adapted to arid coastal bluffs of Greece and North Africa. It is the best choice for arid rocky conditions with less-than-ideal soils.

Lavandula stoechas (Spanish Lavender)

Native of inland Spain, this is the most heat-tolerant lavender species with the largest, most interesting-looking flowers for landscaping in purple hues. This is the most widely used species for warm arid climates.

Botanical Name	Common Name	Height	Zone
Lavandula angustifolia	English Lavender	3' tall and wide	5
Lavandula dentata	French Lavender	5' tall and wide	8
Lavandula stoechas	Spanish Lavender	2' tall and wide	7

LEONOTIS

Leonotis leonurus (Lion's Tail)

Height	Width	Zone	Sun	Bloom Season		Region			Flower Color
5'–6'	4'–5'	8	O	✿	☀	LD	C	IV	Orange

Tall stalks of bright orange flowers are long-blooming on this big, bushy perennial from southern Africa. It is a lover of mild winters and tolerant of extreme inland heat. Foliage is deep olive green, great for contrast against silver or gray foliage. Each whorl of bright orange fades to ball-shaped seed clusters ideal for dried arrangements. In habitat it prefers slopes and higher ground where drainage is rapid to prevent root rot. Such a large, fast-growing perennial is excellent for filling new gardens that feel too bare, or for replacing large shrubs lost to drought. Use it for the back of the dry border, or as a screen, or to insert color into a too-gray setting. It's a perfect companion for succulents and California native shrubs.

PENSTEMON

Height	Width	Zone	Sun	Bloom Season	Region					Flower Color
3'–5'	1'–3'	4–8	○	❀	HD	LD	M	C	IV	Pink, purple, red

California is home to many species of penstemons, one of the most exciting spring flowers for arid gardens. They can be found adapted to the coastal climate all the way up to alpine conditions. It's important to select those best suited to your local microclimate because many readily self-sow if conditions are right, much like a wildflower. In the wild they're often found alone or in small groups on mountain cliffs and foothill cut slopes, or in dry washes or desert canyons where soils are lean and porous. Beware of crowding in the garden, as they prefer to grow singly. Penstemons grow during winter rains, bloom in spring, then die back to dormancy for the summer and fall until rains return. Novices often mistake summer dormancy for dehydration and proceed to water them to death, killing the dormant roots too. Most penstemons are ideal for small spaces because they ask for just a square foot of ground to produce outstanding stalks of vivid flowers. It's wise to check with a local garden center or native plant nursery to determine exactly which species are locally successful and whether they need summer water. With so many species and their many hybrids, you'll find great penstemons in a wide range of hardiness ratings.

Arid Zone Penstemons That Self-Sow

Botanical Name	Common Name	Color	Bloom Height	Zone
Penstemon barbatus	Scarlet Bugler	Red	3'	4
Penstemon eatonii	Firecracker Penstemon	Red	4'	5
Penstemon parryi	Parry Penstemon	Pink	3'	8
Penstemon superbus	Superb Penstemon	Coral	5'	5

PEROVSKIA

Perovskia atriplicifolia (Russian Sage)

Height	Width	Zone	Sun	Bloom Season		Region				Flower Color
3'–4'	3'–4'	5	O	❀	☀	HD	M	C	IV	Violet blue

This beautiful violet-blue-flowered perennial is often used in lieu of tender lavenders to create the same look in colder climates. Heralding from the dry Himalayas, it's easily adapted to almost every western climate zone except the low desert. Be aware that *Perovskia* resents overly fertile soil and prefers rugged naturalistic conditions, and its colors are dulled by overwatering. These plants need a good deal of space, although smaller-stature varieties have been developed that are highly recommended. These are big, outstanding border plants that highlight blue flower color from June through September.

PHLOMIS

Phlomis fruticosa (Jerusalem Sage)

Height	Width	Zone	Sun		Bloom Season		Region					Flower Color
3'–4'	3'–4'	5–8	◑	○	✿	☀	HD	LD	M	C	IV	Yellow

This is one of the most beautiful of all the large Mediterranean perennials and deserves more attention. They are found on rocky eroding slopes where drainage is assured and fertility poor, so don't kill them with kindness. Large gray-green leaves have whitish fuzzy undersides on stems that bear unique whorls of large lemon-yellow flowers that create a truly lovely blend of cool color and texture. A long bloom season extends from early spring deep into summer. *Phlomis* is also far more adaptable than first thought, tolerating much colder winters where it freezes back like a traditional perennial to return from the roots. When grown in mild climates it's evergreen and surprisingly tolerant of low-desert heat but does benefit from protection from direct afternoon sun.

ROMNEYA

Romneya coulteri (Matilija Poppy)

Height	Width	Zone	Sun	Bloom Season	Region					Flower Color
5'	5'	7	O	✿	HD	LD	M	C	IV	White

This may be the largest and most awesome of all California native perennials. It's affectionately called the "fried-egg plant" because the very large white flowers with their golden ball of stamens at the center indeed resemble a fried egg! This poppy is fond of sandy, porous soils where the thick and woody underground stems travel to create colonies of sprouts. It thrives on early winter rains, producing tall, upright blue-green stems with terminal blooms from spring into summer, then the whole plant dies back for the dry season. Even though the poppy is native to coastal foothills, it's far more heat tolerant, growing happily in the low desert under irrigation. This plant is an excellent problem solver for high ground, hillside sites, cut slopes, and wherever soils are lean and well drained.

SALVIA

The salvias for dry gardens are not those eastern species you see in most plant catalogs. Those that thrive on minimal water originate in the Southwest and Mexico where conditions are distinctly arid. These can be classified as subshrubs because they develop a woody base that is long lived. They are somewhat perennial too because the softer herbaceous flowering growth can be renewed by hard pruning annually to maintain long-term vigor. Some will bloom all summer long and may flower nearly year-round where there's little frost. Their main weakness is too much water, which causes root rot, so it's best to err on the side of too dry rather than risk losing the plant. These are the workhorses of your garden, so plant many and try all the different forms to learn which works best where you live.

Salvia greggii (Autumn Sage)

Height	Width	Zone	Sun		Bloom Season			Region			Flower Color
2'–3'	2'–3'	7	◑	○	✿	☀	⚜	LD	C	IV	Red, hybrids variable

This native perennial of the Southwest and Mexico is the best source of heat and drought-resistant color well tested in the furnace of the low desert. The species is red flowered and so are some of the hybrids such as 'Furman's Red', which is hardier to Zone 6. These are without question the biggest hummingbird draws of all. Birds claim their plants and defend them vigorously. Newer hybrids and sports have brought in pinks and purples and white, with some bicolored such as white and coral 'Hot Lips'.

Salvia greggii 'Stormy Pink'

Salvia microphylla 'Hot Lips'

Salvia greggii 'Ultra Violet'

Salvia leucantha 'Mexican Bush Sage'

Salviai 'Allen Chickering'

Salviai 'Allen Chickering'

Salvia leucantha (Mexican Bush Sage)

Height	Width	Zone	Sun		Bloom Season		Region		Flower Color
4'–5'	3'–4'	9	◑	○	✽	☀	LD	C	Purple

Hailing from warm tropical regions of Mexico, this sage is best where marine influence moderates inland summer heat. It is a useful large-stature perennial that fills empty spaces in the garden with dense, fast growth. Long velvety purple flower stems rise above linear aromatic, gray-tinged foliage. Fast-growing, it should be cut back in early winter to encourage fresh new growth with the coming rains. While not as drought resistant as the other sages, it is a fine plant for drip irrigation in gravel gardens or for background in Mediterranean landscapes and as fillers in succulent compositions.

Salvia 'Allen Chickering' (Cleveland Sage)

Height	Width	Zone	Sun	Bloom Season		Region					Flower Color
3'–4'	3'–4'	8	○	✽	☀	HD	LD	M	C	IV	Purple

This very western sage is a hybrid of California native *Salvia clevelandii* and purple sage, *Salvia leucophylla*. This is a plant quite capable of naturalizing in many areas where it may survive most of the summer without supplemental watering. Rangy and wide, its foliage is redolent with the earthy scent of soil blended with culinary sage. Its stiff wands rise above leaves bearing segmented whorls of lavender flowers. These fade to ball-shaped seedpods that are favorites of small birds and can be cut to make fine dried-arrangement material for use indoors. This plant is easily overwatered if not grown in dry circumstances, but it's the quintessential choice for grouping with matilija poppy and brittlebush.

SANTOLINA

Santolina chamaecyparissus (Lavender Cotton)

Height	Width	Zone	Sun		Bloom Season	Region				Flower Color
12"	2'–3'	6	◐	○	✿	HD	LD	C	IV	Yellow

These tidy little mounds of dense, fuzzy gray aromatic foliage hail from the Mediterranean region where they were cultivated in medieval knot gardens, demonstrating a tolerance of regular clipping. A lover of warm, dry conditions and fast-draining, low-fertility soils, they are perfectly tailored to smaller arid gardens that need plants in scale with the space. *Santolina* blooms with profuse small yellow daisies in spring, then should be shorn back to its original form. Whether grown as individuals or in groups for more visibility in larger gardens, they will demand full sun and resent overwatering. A less common species that is equally drought resistant, *Santolina virens*, is identical but with deep-green foliage. Try planting these two in a checkerboard pattern of green and gray to lend an old-world formal composition to Mediterranean architecture gardens.

STACHYS

Stachys byzantina (Lamb's Ear)

Height	Width	Zone	Sun	Bloom Season	Region				Flower Color
6"–12"	2'–3'	4	◑	✤	HD	M	C	IV	Purple

This fuzzy-leaf perennial originates in the lands of the Byzantine Empire of western Asia where conditions are cold and dry. It's a fine choice for high desert and mountain regions as well as drier inland regions because it is vulnerable to fungal diseases caused by summer humidity. What makes it so charming is a low-growing habit of whitish 4-inch-long animal ear–shaped leaves for small groundcover patches. Plants will spread by runners into larger colonies that are popular edging for pathways and in the foreground of perennial borders. In summer, curious fuzzy flower spikes rise a foot above the foliage, bearing whorls of small purple flowers. While lamb's ear is a full sun plant, it should have afternoon shade inland and in the desert. This is an outstanding cold-hardy dryland plant for foothill and mountain locations of the inland West.

ZAUSCHNERIA OR *EPILOBIUM*

Zauschneria californica (California Fuchsia)

Height	Width	Zone	Sun	Bloom Season		Region			Flower Color
12"–18"	2'–3'	8	O	🪷	☀	M	C	IV	Red orange

Vigorous and vivid, this beautiful little perennial is the quintessential rock garden plant that thrives with little to no summer water once naturalized. Thin, brittle stems and grayish foliage give rise to 2-inch-long, orange-red fuchsia-like flowers for bold summer color. It's renowned for the sheer quantity of blooms highly appealing to hummingbirds. These plants are spreaders by underground roots into large colonies. This is problematic in smaller gardens if the plant is not given boundaries, but in large open dry landscapes this expanding coverage is desirable. Breeders are crossing this species with other western *Zauschneria* to create many new and

improved hybrids listed under this genus or the synonym, *Epilobium canum*. Though small to start, this will become a big plant that is a perfect fit with *Salvia* 'Allen Chickering' and matilija poppy, which all resent much or any summer water.

Five High-Heat Low-Desert Perennials

1. *Gaura lindheimeri* (Gaura)

2. *Salvia greggii* (Autumn Sage)

3. *Encelia farinosa* (Brittlebush, Incienso)

4. *Penstemon parryi* (Parry Penstemon)

5. *Euphorbia rigida* (Gopher Plant)

Five Big Fillers for New Gardens or Barren Spots

Botanical Name	Common Name	Flower Color
Encelia farinosa	Brittlebush, Incienso	Golden yellow
Leonotis leonurus	Lion's Tail	Orange
Phlomis fruticosa	Jerusalem Sage	Yellow
Romneya coulteri	Matilija Poppy	White
Salvia leucantha	Mexican Bush Sage	Purple

Five Gray or Pubescent Foliage

1. *Encelia farinosa* (Brittlebush, Incienso)

2. *Lavandula dentata* (French Lavender)

3. *Perovskia atriplicifolia* (Russian Sage)

4. *Santolina chamaecyparissus* (Lavender Cotton)

5. *Stachys byzantina* (Lamb's Ear)

Five California Native Perennials

1. *Encelia farinosa* (Brittlebush, Incienso)

2. *Penstemon* hybrids (Penstemon)

3. *Romneya coulteri* (Matilija Poppy)

4. *Salvia* 'Allen Chickering' (Cleveland Sage)

5. *Zauschneria/Epilobium* (California Fuchsia)

Five Hot Hummingbird Flowers

1. *Kniphofia uvaria* (Red Hot Poker, Torch Lily)

2. *Leonotis leonurus* (Lion's Tail)

3. *Penstemon* hybrids (Penstemon)

4. *Salvia greggii* (Autumn Sage)

5. *Zauschneria/Epilobium* (California Fuchsia)

Perennial Selection Matrix

BOTANICAL NAME	COMMON NAME	ZONE	HEIGHT	WIDTH	COLORS
Achillea millefolium	Yarrow	3	2'	1'–2'	Yellow, variable
Convolvulus cneorum	Bush Morning Glory, Silverbush	8	2'–4'	2'–4'	White
Dietes vegeta a.k.a. *Moraea iridioides*	Fortnight Lily	8	3'–4'	3'–4'	White
*Encelia farinosa**	Brittlebush, Incienso	8	2'–3'	2'–3'	Golden yellow
Euphorbia rigida	Gopher Plant	7	2'	3'	Yellow
Gaura lindheimeri	Gaura	5	3'–4'	4'–5'	White, pink
Kniphofia uvaria	Red Hot Poker, Torch Lily	7	2'–3'	2'–3'	Red orange
Lavandula angustifolia	English Lavender	5	3'	3'	Blue
Lavandula dentata	French Lavender	8	5'	5'	Blue
Leonotis leonurus	Lion's Tail	8	5'–6'	4'–5'	Orange
Lavandula stoechas	Spanish Lavender	7	2'	2'	Purple blue
Penstemon hybrids*	Penstemon	4–8	3'–5'	1'–3'	Pink, purple, red
Perovskia atriplicifolia	Russian Sage	5	3'–4'	3'–4'	Violet blue
Phlomis fruticosa	Jerusalem Sage	5–8	3'–4'	3'–4'	Yellow
*Romneya coulteri**	Matilija Poppy	7	5'	5'	White
Salvia greggii	Autumn Sage	7	2'–3'	2'–3'	Reds, hybrids variable
Salvia leucantha	Mexican Bush Sage	9	4'–5'	3'–4'	Purple
Salvia 'Allen Chickering'*	Cleveland Sage	8	3'–4'	3'–4'	Purple
Santolina chamaecyparissus	Lavender Cotton	6	12"	2'–3'	Yellow
Stachys byzantina	Lamb's Ear	4	6"–12"	2'–3'	Purple
*Zauschneria californica**	California Fuchsia	8	12"–18"	2'–3'	Red orange

*Indicates California native species.

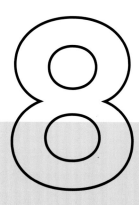

Animated Plants and Fine Textures

When winds ruffle the tall grasses of the American prairie, this amazing plant community literally comes alive. Grasses also flow over coastal dunes like waves of fine foliage. Shorter mesic or dry prairie grasses provide durable erosion control for the challenging hot, dry winds of the Southwest. Huge saw grasses dominate the landscapes of the wet Southeast. Not all these wild grasses are suited to arid zone gardens, but those that do flower well and offer bright color and exciting forms.

Design with ornamental grasses is popular because they bloom in late summer and fall when most gardens experience a lull in flowering. Purple fountain grass or pink muhly offer beautiful colored flowers that are real standouts in the autumn garden. But there's a more important reason to integrate grasses into flower gardens: diversity.

In Southern California, fountain grass, *Pennisetum setaceum*, and its cultivars have become plantas non grata because they so easily naturalize due to lack of frost. As a result, windblown seed from landscaping invades wildland plant communities to displace native grasses and their kin. Before planting ornamental grasses in homes adjacent to wildland open space, flood plains, undeveloped land, parks, and preserves, determine whether any candidate is listed on your state's invasive species criteria. This ensures you don't inadvertently contaminate pristine wildlands with exotic grasses.

This group with its curious wind-pollinated blossoms is the counterbalance to all the hard architectural succulents, rocks, and gravel. They make a garden richer because it's not limited to beauty in one or two seasons. In warmer climates where fall color in deciduous trees and shrubs is rare, the grasses literally carry the season until the winter solstice cold descends. They're left in flower for winter interests where it's cold, then cut back to just a few inches at the close of winter. This exposes the crown or base of the grass to direct sun to encourage new spring shoots to flourish into a clean, new fluffy mass of green. Moreover, the lushness of these arid zone grasses balances out the loss of greenery as water-loving plants die out during drought.

How Grasses Work in a Dry Garden

Prairie: A prairie is a plant community composed of both grasses and perennials. The tallgrass prairie of the northern plains is the most famous example with its huge grasses and native flowers depending on extensive summer rainfall and deep fertile soils. Farther south is the mesic prairie, a similar community using grasses and perennials with more annual wildflowers. The mesic prairie is a much better model and plant palette for drought-prone regions.

Meadow: Meadows are often found in mountain regions or where the land is heavily forested. Meadows are the last stage of succession from lakes that gradually fill in with silt until they are so shallow that grasses thrive there. This application is best for cooler coastal and mountain regions.

Masses: In regions where lawns are being removed to reduce water consumption, fields of larger ornamental grasses are used along with other plants to fill these spaces. Massing also includes the use of grasses on rigid grids to complement the clean lines of modern architecture. Masses tend to be monocultural, but it's more sustainable to blend various grasses rather than a single species.

Grouping: Natural groupings is the most common way to use ornamental grasses. They appear to pop up serendipitously in nature, with irregular spacing, combined with boulders for a simple effect or blended into more diverse plantings to add late-season volume, color, and movement to otherwise static plantings.

Individual: At maturity some grasses can reach large proportions, which allow them to be used as individuals. This is helpful in small-space gardens where a single large grass takes on a new role as a textural and upright focal point with seasonal color. A single grass in a well-selected pot, or a series of them, can result in outstanding accents in gardens where breezes keep the flower heads swaying on a terrace, patio, balcony, or deck.

Well-Proven Ornamental Grasses for Dry Gardens

Key

Sun			Bloom Season				Region				
●	◐	○	✿	☀	🍁	❄	HD	LD	M	C	IV
SHADE	PARTLY SUNNY	SUN	SPRING	SUMMER	FALL	WINTER	HIGH DESERT	LOW DESERT	MOUN-TAINS	COAST	INLAND VALLEY

Grasses constitute one of the largest plant families on Earth and most appear similar. It can be tough to tell them apart. It's important to realize that most grasses, no matter how beautiful, are not drought-resistant plants. Without plentiful moisture they fail to achieve their proper stature, foliage, and coloring. Over the years a few have proven themselves in heat and drought to be amazingly beautiful and resilient. They are also long-lived, an important criteria for plants used in a landscape.

TIP: Ornamental grasses that are the most drought-resistant bear fine needle-thin foliage to reduce the amount of surface area vulnerable to moisture loss. Wide-leaf grasses and similar cultivars of any drought-resistant species will require more moisture.

FESTUCA GLAUCA (BLUE FESCUE)

Height	Width	Zone	Sun	Bloom Season		Region					Flower Color
12"	12"	4	O	⚘	🍁	HD	LD	M	C	IV	White

Because diminutive blue fescue is native to southern France, it's the ideal choice for blending with drought-resistant Mediterraneans such as lavender and *Santolina*. In the 1960s, this was a favorite grass of midcentury modern homes and Japanese-influenced gardens, so it fits nicely into that vintage palette. Very cold hardy, this plant is ideal for mountains and foothill areas where soils are well drained. They do not tolerate saturated ground during the winter, so grow them in raised planting areas or on mild slopes where drainage is assured. This is a perfect grass for blending with cold-hardy alpine succulents such as *Sedum* and *Sempervivum* in poor rocky ground. To maintain a more tidy dome-like form in modern geometric

plantings, gardeners often snip off the flower heads as soon as they form. Allowing flower heads to remain lends a wholly different naturalistic character to rock gardens or maximizes fine texture contrast among rigid succulents. The variety 'Boulder Blue' is highly recommended for mountain regions.

ANIMATED PLANTS AND FINE TEXTURES

MUHLENBERGIA CAPILLARIS 'REGAL MIST' (PINK MUHLY)

Height	Width	Zone	Sun	Bloom Season		Region					Flower Color
3'	3'	6	O	☀	⚜	HD	LD	M	C	IV	Pink

This species of muhly produces naturally pink-tinged flowers, but selected varieties such as 'Regal Mist' have bold magenta inflorescences for late season when many native plants are dormant in the West. Flowering peaks during fall from September to the holidays. This standout is used as an accent in residential gardens where it blends in with succulent plantings along the coast, making a less invasive option there than fountain grass. This is also a well-proven match for yucca and other rigid desert plants farther inland, and a superior rock garden candidate because of its adaptation to sandy, gravelly soils in which it becomes a beautiful problem solver for the irregular terrain of mountains and foothills.

MUHLENBERGIA RIGENS (DEERGRASS)

Height	Width	Zone	Sun	Bloom Season	Region					Flower Color
					HD	LD	M	C	IV	
3'	4'	6–7	O	🍁	HD	LD	M	C	IV	Beige

There's no question that deergrass will prove a useful drought-resistant plant, as it's the most common native species for dry Arizona and is also found in wildlands of Nevada, New Mexico, and Texas, as well as Mexico. Narrow leaves in a spherical form produce equally fine pinnate flower stalks, which provide a semitransparent appearance with little problem litter for swimming pools and water features. In cultivated gardens there's a uniformity of growth to this grass that has made it a popular yet simple linear planting choice along driveways that takes heat reflected off paving. There is no better large grass for a naturalistic rock garden or dry streambed or for grid planting in modern landscapes.

NASSELLA TENUISSIMA (MEXICAN FEATHER GRASS)

Height	Width	Zone	Sun		Bloom Season	Region			Flower Color
18"	18"	6	◑	○	☼	LD	C	IV	Beige

The finest textured of all ornamental grasses, this species native to Texas and New Mexico as well as Mexico and Argentina is often described as hairlike or feathery. Shorter stature to just 2 feet tall, it is a fine choice for smaller gardens where most other grasses are too large and overwhelming. Feathery flowers rise in summer to add a softer texture to this already superfine element. Grow against rigid rocks and boulders to glorify the contrast. It's super popular for blending with aloes and other succulents that share similar water requirements in both small-scale and large mass plantings.

PENNISETUM SETACEUM (GREEN FOUNTAIN GRASS)

Height	Width	Zone	Sun	Bloom Season		Region			Flower Color
3'	3'	9	○	☀	🍁	LD	C	IV	Beige

This is a tropical African grass that is frost tender, so it's treated like an annual everywhere but frost-free or nearly frost-free zones of the Pacific Coast where it is an invasive problem plant. It is named for the beautiful arching, pendulous lavender and pink-tone flower spikes that nod and sway in the slightest breeze over darker green linear foliage. In bloom there is no more beautiful ornamental grass. In mild Southern California these grasses self-sow, releasing prodigious seed into gardens, which makes it potentially weedy under broadcast irrigation. They naturalize readily in these mild regions too, creating problems for native vegetation in coastal dunes and inland wetlands. Beware of planting upwind from a swimming pool or water feature, as fluffy seed heads disintegrate in the wind and can be difficult to remove from water.

TIP: Though not as drought tolerant as tender fountain grass, its Asian cousin, *Pennisetum alopecuroides*, shares similar appearance and thrives in cold winters of Zone 6. It's an ideal plant for gardeners in the higher elevations of the Intermountain West.

PENNISETUM SETACEUM 'RUBRUM'
(PURPLE FOUNTAIN GRASS)

Height	Width	Zone	Sun	Bloom Season		Region			Flower Color
3'	18"	8	O	☼	🍁	LD	C	IV	Purple

This variation on the species is a much-loved purple-leaf form that is the highlight of
autumn gardens. An upright grower, it will reach 5 feet at maturity over a single long
season, providing quick fillers and visual interest early on in a new landscape when
slower plants are still small. Very tender, it prefers locations where temperatures don't
drop below 40 degrees F; elsewhere it's treated as a long-lived annual. This variety
rarely sets seed, so it will not be weedy in the garden nor in the wild, which makes
it a better choice than the species *P. setaceum*, where invasiveness is a problem. The
variety 'Eaton Canyon' is a dwarf red form that does not exceed 30 inches, making it
an excellent choice for smaller spaces.

Five Companions for Meadow and Prairie Gardens

Botanical Name	Common Name	Flower Color
Muhlenbergia rigens	Deergrass	Beige
Achillea millefolium	Fernleaf Yarrow	Many
Perovskia atriplicifolia	Russian Sage	Violet blue
Coreopsis spp.	Tickseed	Yellow
Eschscholzia californica	California Poppy	Yellow orange

Five Companions for Wild and Rock Gardens

Botanical Name	Common Name	Flower Color
Nassella tenuissima	Mexican Feather Grass	Beige
Pennisetum setaceum	Green Fountain Grass	Beige
Gaura lindheimeri	Gaura	White, pink
Salvia greggii hybrids	Autumn Sage	Varies
Zauschneria californica	California Fuchsia	Red orange

Five Companions for Modern Gardens

Botanical Name	Common Name	Flower Color
Festuca glauca	Blue Fescue	White
Kniphofia uvaria	Red Hot Poker, Torch Lily	Red orange
Stachys byzantina	Lamb's Ear	Purple
Euphorbia rigida	Gopher Plant	Yellow
Agave americana	Blue Agave	Bronze

Five Companions for Color Gardens

Botanical Name	Common Name	Flower Color
Festuca glauca	Blue Fescue	White
Muhlenbergia capillaris 'Regal Mist'	Pink Muhly	Pink
Pennisetum setaceum 'Rubrum'	Purple Fountain Grass	Purple
Delosperma cooperi	Iceplant	Varies
Cistus 'Sunset'	Hybrid Rockrose	Dark pink

Grasslike Plants

Many plants are often mistaken for grasses but are very different plants both in their needs and origins. In the dry garden they offer a wide range of textural alternatives that function like grasses in the landscape, but they're much hardier, some are succulent, and some can even live in both water or on dry land. Consider each of these as a unique individual.

ASCLEPIAS SUBULATA (DESERT MILKWEED)

Height	Width	Zone	Sun	Bloom Season	Region	Flower Color
4'	2'	9	○	✿	LD	Cream

Widespread concern for monarch butterfly habitat has brought this desert-hardy beauty out of the shadows. A transparent collection of bluish stiff stems is topped in spring with small creamy blossoms rich in nectar. This plant looks great all the time and its pale coloring is visually pleasant, blending into subshrubs and perennials or spotted into rocky streambeds with extreme drainage. For greatest benefit to the monarchs, plant it in groups to maximize flower access with minimal energy demands to reach them.

CHONDROPETALUM TECTORUM (CAPE RUSH)

Height	Width	Zone	Sun	Bloom Season	Region			Flower Color
3'	3'	8	O	☀	LD	C	IV	Brown

This great-looking reed is a frost-tender South African from the Cape region and thus thrives in the similar Pacific Coast maritime climate. Composed of beautiful wiry stiff mounds of fine-textured foliage, these are accented by rusty-colored reproductive structures. These plants look super in containers. Plant them alone to emphasize their hemispherical shape and fine-textured semitransparency. In ground it's a great focal point increased by massing plants around boulders and dotted into drainage swale dry streambeds. This plant should never be cut back or divided as with grasses, but removal of dead material resulting from frost damage is the exception.

DASYLIRION LONGISSIMUM (MEXICAN GRASS TREE)

Height	Width	Zone	Sun	Bloom Season		Region		Flower Color
4'	5'	8	O	🏵	☼	HD	LD	Beige

This living version of the modern wire "starburst" sculpture offers a work of art in the garden. Composed of wirelike leaves that are stiff on a very symmetrical plant, it brings unique geometry and rigid texture into contemporary landscapes. Few other plants look so great in a field of fine gravel or lighted so their narrow shadow patterns play on a wall or building surface. This slow-growing plant takes a long time to reach its ideal form, so it's worth paying more for older specimens that look much better in the short term. Long-lived, this plant begins as a foliage hemisphere, then, as it develops a trunk over time, the shape becomes more spherical. Like most of its kind this is a widely adaptable species provided there is plenty of sun and soils are well drained. Use safety glasses when weeding or trimming this plant.

DASYLIRION WHEELERI (DESERT SPOON, SOTOL)

Height	Width	Zone	Sun	Bloom Season		Region		Flower Color
4'	4'	6	O	✿	☀	HD	LD	Cream

These big balls of beautiful light-gray tooth-edged foliage are symmetrical enough to work wonders in modern design, offering all the texture and transparency of grasses without any of the mess. Native to the desert Southwest and Mexico, they prefer gravelly hillsides in middle-elevation foothills and are quite capable of withstanding snow and the dry winter cold of mountain regions. This plant flowers every year or so with a tall stalk rising to 12 feet, with dramatic May to July bloom. There is no greater accent for iron-stained stone or boulders. Do not plant close to pool decks.

HESPERALOE PARVIFLORA (RED YUCCA)

Height	Width	Zone	Sun	Bloom Season		Region			Flower Color
3'	4'	7	○	✿	☀	HD	LD	IV	Coral red

This is one of the most versatile perennials from the desert palette because it's so widely adaptable elsewhere. Hailing from southwest Texas and northern Mexico, it was considered the "western aloe" because flowers are coral red, tubular, and held on a tall stem much like that of the African aloes. Its narrow rolled leaves in an upright clump lack spines or thorns, so they are ideal for pedestrian areas and swimming pools. *Hesperaloe* is almost always planted in groups where the many stalks maximize its visibility when in flower. These have been used in geometric layouts as well as for modern landscapes. It is believed that under the right conditions plants may prove more cold hardy and will adapt to a wide range of soils and reflected heat from paving and walls. A creamy yellow-flowered form is available but less commonly seen.

PEDILANTHUS MACROCARPUS (SLIPPER PLANT)

Height	Width	Zone	Sun		Bloom Season	Region		Flower Color
3'	2'	10	◑	○	✿	LD	C	Coral red

Despite its origins in the Sonoran Desert, *Pedilanthus* is remarkably adaptable to more hospitable conditions. These pencil-sized rods of plant are a beautiful celadon color because of the whitish tinge to its skin. But what makes its unruly hoard of rods striking are bright coral blossoms at the tops. In the wild this plant begins life under a nurse plant, anything from a cholla to a paloverde. They become established protected from sun and wind by the nurse plant. This tells us it wants light shade, particularly in the summer afternoons.

SANSEVIERIA TRIFASCIATA (MOTHER-IN-LAW'S TONGUE, SNAKE PLANT)

Height	Width	Zone	Sun		Bloom Season	Region		Flower Color
3'	18"	10	●	◑	☀	LD	C	Cream

This ubiquitous houseplant is a super outdoor accent in frost-free climates or when grown outside in the summer. It's a tropical African species well adapted to the long dry season there. It's not at all frost hardy nor does it tolerate direct sun inland. There are many hybrids of this and other *Sansevieria* species that are taller, shorter, lighter, and darker for a variety of hues. They work well in dark spots such as slots between buildings, and they thrive in the desert under the shelter of trees and patio covers. On the coast they love full sun in the maritime climate. This is a signature plant of midcentury architecture, often used indoors for accents or room dividers when planted in long narrow troughs.

Animated Plants Selection Matrix

BOTANICAL NAME	COMMON NAME	ZONE	FOLIAGE COLOR	GROUP
*Asclepias subulata**	Desert Milkweed	9	Blue green	Succulent
Chondropetalum tectorum	Cape Rush	8	Olive green	Reed
Dasylirion longissimum	Mexican Grass Aloe Tree	8	Green	Succulent
Dasylirion wheeleri	Desert Spoon, Sotol	6	Blue green	Succulent
Festuca glauca	Blue Fescue	4	Blue	Grass
Hesperaloe parviflora	Red Yucca	7	Olive green	Succulent
Muhlenbergia capillaris 'Regal Mist'	Pink Muhly	6	Green	Grass
*Muhlenbergia rigens**	Deergrass	6–7	Green	Grass
Nassella tenuissima	Mexican Feather Grass	6	Light green	Grass
Pedilanthus macrocarpus	Slipper Plant	10	Blue green	Succulent
Pennisetum setaceum	Green Fountain Grass	9	Green	Grass
Pennisetum setaceum 'Rubrum'	Purple Fountain Grass	9	Burgundy	Grass
Sanseveria trifasciata	Mother-in-Law's Tongue, Snake Plant	10	Green, yellow	Succulent

*Indicates California native species.

9 The Canopy

Flowering trees are real attention getters at home and out in the community. Many areas are defined by their flowering street trees that are usually selected for high compatibility with the local climate. Trees that are suited to the new drier West are many, but few offer a vivid floral show as these do. They are unusual examples of how to blend shade and seasonal color in the dry garden.

About Drought-Resistant Tree Roots

Tree species native to the dry regions of the world defy aridity to survive under minimal rainfall. To do so they often compensate by evolving large, wide, or deep and expansive root systems to capture water trapped far underground. These roots can't distinguish between natural moisture and that of plumbing, sewers, swimming pools, and other water sources. Plant one in your yard and in no time it will dominate everything above- and belowground. It's the natural root vigor that allows them to survive, but this characteristic is potentially damaging to paving, foundations, and other constructed elements. However, the trees listed in this chapter are not considered aggressively rooted unless indicated.

Before You Marry . . . Know Them Well

Planting a tree is like getting married, and we all know that getting hitched to a stranger is not a good idea no matter how beautiful he or she may be. Choosing trees to bring excitement, beauty, and color into your yard requires full knowledge of the candidate. With so many years required for any tree to reach maturity, you can't afford a divorce because it takes another lifetime to start all over again.

> **Deciduous:** Most flowering trees are deciduous, losing their leaves for winter dormancy. This suits passive solar design for bringing light and solar heating into a home on the south-side windows during the winter months. This heats interior spaces naturally and may also contribute to fall color.
>
> ....
>
> **Shape and Form:** The shape or form of a tree is its silhouette at maturity, which dictates how it functions in the landscape. Do not rely on how a young container-grown tree looks at the garden center because it may change form a number of times before maturity.
>
> ....
>
> **Litter:** All trees generate litter, but flowering trees are likely to create more litter of a different kind. Every flower will fade and drop off, creating a mess beneath the canopy of flower parts and in some cases fruit that follows. Beware of this litter on patios, sidewalks, and driveways to avoid problems with autos and pedestrian safety.
>
> ....

Leaf Size: The size and shape of a tree's leaf can have an impact on the density of its shade. It's also a big deal with swimming pools because compound leaves tend to disintegrate in the water. They are nearly impossible to skim and must be vacuumed.

....

Local Climate: Even though a tree may grow well in your USDA Plant Hardiness Zone, beware of your immediate microclimate that may enhance or discourage the growth rate of a new tree. The best way to verify the choice is to drive around older neighborhoods to see if any mature specimens can be found.

....

Will It Fit?

Always visualize any tree at three-fourths mature size when placing it in a planting design. That tree must fit exactly into the space provided and serve the function required. A known dimension for the diameter of the canopy at maturity tells you if it will provide enough shade or perhaps too much. Knowing height tells you if it will block second-story views or screen the neighbor's basketball hoop.

Plan Irrigation Accordingly

Drought changes how we water trees. In the past spray irrigation was fine, but today we're growing trees on drip systems that deliver water in a very different way. Always begin your tree with drip irrigation so it becomes adapted that way from day one. Be prepared to hand water over the first dry season to help it through extreme heat or hot winds.

TIP: Know where your utilities are before you plant a tree. Keep well away from power lines, water, sewer, and septic and leach fields so that neither canopy nor roots will cause problems in the future. Many areas have programs where the utility companies will come out and mark their lines in your yard before you embark on digging projects.

THE CANOPY

Flowering Trees for Drought

Key

Sun			Bloom Season				Region				
●	◐	○	✽	☀	🍁	❄	HD	LD	M	C	IV
SHADE	PARTLY SUNNY	SUN	SPRING	SUMMER	FALL	WINTER	HIGH DESERT	LOW DESERT	MOUN-TAINS	COAST	INLAND VALLEY

ACACIA BAILEYANA 'PURPUREA' (BAILEY'S ACACIA)

Height	Width	Zone	Sun	Bloom Season	Region		Flower Color	Type
30'	20'	7	○	✽	C	IV	Yellow	Ever-green

While many acacias are among our best drought trees, they have become a serious allergy problem in many areas where they grow in abundance. Therefore only the most beautiful of them is featured here— the species that features attractive bluish fernlike leaves with new growth tinted purple with this cultivar. The contrast of canary-yellow spring flowers with blue-and-purple foliage makes it pop in the spring. This acacia tends to produce multiple trunks for a naturalistic mass that's ideal for backgrounds and evergreen screens. If you prefer a tidier look, choose a standard single trunk and shape a canopy with annual pruning. The result is more dense growth and foliage color visibility all year, followed by the bloom show that gives this canopy a casual pendulous character.

ALBIZIA JULIBRISSIN (MIMOSA)

Height	Width	Zone	Sun	Bloom Season	Region		Flower Color	Type
20'–40'	30'	6	O	✿	LD	IV	Pink	Deciduous

From the cold, dry region of Asia Minor comes a large super-drought-resistant tree that is at once incredibly beautiful and messy. Light fernlike foliage produces an open canopy that is in a perpetual state of change. In spring it blooms with decidedly feminine-pink powder puff blossoms, which mature into large seedpods. When these mature they fall too, for phase two of litter. Finally in the fall when trees go dormant, the leaves finish off this three-part litter schedule. However, for larger properties where you need a big tree to do the job of both beauty and shade, this is a great choice. Nothing makes a better long-range focal point for rural homes for shading large open spaces. Keep well away from pools, water gardens, outdoor living spaces, and rooflines.

ARBUTUS UNEDO (STRAWBERRY TREE)

Height	Width	Zone	Sun	Bloom Season		Region		Flower Color	Type
25'	25'	8	O	✿	☀	C	IV	White	Evergreen

For those in the West who love the hard-to-grow native madrone trees, this Mediterranean is a visually similar relative that makes a great look-alike. Peeling bark and large clusters of small bell-shaped flowers yield to marble-sized, bumpy, bright red fruit. Strawberry-sized fruits stand out brightly against dark green foliage. It's a slow to moderate grower best for smaller yards along the coast and in milder inland valleys, and it's a perfect choice for acidic soils of redwood, fir, and pine forest homesites.

BAUHINIA × BLAKEANA (HONG KONG ORCHID TREE)

Height	Width	Zone	Sun	Bloom Season	Region		Flower Color	Type
25'	20'	9	○	✿	LD	C	Pink	Deciduous

This incredibly gorgeous deciduous tree hails from China where it was discovered 100 years ago growing in the ruins of an old house outside Hong Kong. This one tree was different—it is believed to be a natural hybrid of two native *Bauhinia* that have found their way into warm climate gardens to become rather weedy and invasive. The problem with the species is they are fast, almost rank growing, and they produce copious litter and seedlings that pop up everywhere. So naturally when this seed-free sterile hybrid was discovered it became the most desirable form propagated vegetatively all over the world. Always ask for the "sterile hybrid" to make sure you get the clean, brightly colored, large-flowered, and well-behaved tree of exceptional tropical beauty.

CHILOPSIS LINEARIS (DESERT WILLOW)

Height	Width	Zone	Sun	Bloom Season	Region			Flower Color	Type
20'–30'	20'	7	O	✿	HD	LD	IV	Pink	Deciduous

This tree of southwestern desert dry washes may be one of the most underestimated flowering trees for arid zone homes. Adapted to searing heat and seasonal water, its linear foliage produces tons of shell-pink flowers, each resembling a single snapdragon blossom. This is a great flowering problem solver for very poor granular soils or rocky ground. As a Southwest desert native, this tree is able to withstand minimal irrigation and extreme inland heat as well as snow and high winds. It is an exceptional choice for local native bees as well as honeybees that flock to its nectar. Rabbits love the fallen spring blossoms and dine on the seed in late summer.

CHITALPA × TASHKENTENSIS (CHITALPA)

Height	Width	Zone	Sun	Bloom Season		Region				Flower Color	Type
20'–30'	20'–30'	6	O	⌘	☀	HD	LD	M	IV	Pale pink	Deciduous

Seeking a more cold-hardy desert willow, breeders managed a rare intergeneric hybrid that is proving one of the best-ever trees for heat and drought. They crossed American Desert Willow, *Chilopsis linearis*, with cold-hardy *Catalpa bignonioides* to improve hardiness. The result is a much more civilized desert willow that lacks the ranginess and litter with larger leaves and flowers. These trees always stand out in the arid regions because they don't look like drought trees. This is the perfect choice for an urban yard seeking traditional flowers without increasing water demand. With hardiness to well below zero, this is a great tree for foothill and mountain homes.

CHORISIA SPECIOSA (SILK FLOSS TREE)

Height	Width	Zone	Sun	Bloom Season	Region		Flower Color	Type
40'–60'	20'–30'	9	O	✿	LD	C	Magenta	Decidiuous

This elegant beauty of South America is famous for its large magenta flowers that resemble those of orchid trees. They are gathered high in the canopy for easy pollination protected by a trunk lined with big stout thorns that are amazing at close range. This character is finding a home in modern gardens seeking a single defining architectural tree. Though just barely frost hardy, this tree is often found in low-desert gardens or along the south Pacific Coast. Because of frequent drought in its homeland, these trees evolved to stand periods of extreme dryness and heat, surviving to flourish again when the rains return.

JACARANDA ACUTIFOLIA (JACARANDA)

Height	Width	Zone	Sun	Bloom Season	Region		Flower Color	Type
50'	30'	9	O	✿	LD	C	Purple	Deciduous

When the Los Angeles jacarandas are in spring bloom, whole neighborhoods become lavender wonderlands. This South American tree has been planted all over the world, wherever conditions are warm enough to support it. Deciduous with large fernlike leaves, its fast growth, drought resistance, and lack of any major pests or diseases makes it a great tree for larger homesites. At maturity this tree can reach huge proportions and is all too often hacked back to strengthen branching and limit overall size, which actually only makes them weaker. When growing naturally on larger homesites or commercial landscapes, this tree is beyond comparison in beauty, speed of growth, and color for frost-free zones.

LAGERSTROEMIA INDICA HYBRIDS (CRAPE MYRTLE)

Height	Width	Zone	Sun	Bloom Season	Region				Flower Color	Type
25'–30'	25'	7	O	☼	HD	LD	M	IV	Pinks, white, red, lavender	Deciduous

Crape myrtle is a favorite of the south where its blooms are often the only color in the dead heat and humidity. However, this tree is equally suited to the arid western states where it has proven itself up and down the Pacific Coast. Its only drawback is a tendency to mildew on the immediate coast. Surprisingly able to withstand heat and drought, minimal irrigation, and heavy soils, these make some of the best trees for small city and suburban gardens. With so many hybrids, it's important to distinguish these shade tree–sized crapes from the much smaller shrubby hybrids. The US National Arboretum breeding program has developed a series of improved, mildew-resistant varieties that make better coastal choices. Crape myrtles, with their multitone bark and sinuous limbs, are exceptional patio shade trees that won't take over or produce a lot of litter.

US Arboretum Hybrids—Crape Myrtle Color and Height Guide

Varietal Name	Flower Color	Height
'Biloxi'	Pale pink	25'
'Choctaw'	Bright pink	30'
'Kiowa'	White	30'
'Miami'	Dark pink	25'
'Muskogee'	Lavender	30'
'Natchez'	White	30'

PARKINSONIA FLORIDA (BLUE PALOVERDE)

Height	Width	Zone	Sun	Bloom Season	Region		Flower Color	Type
20'	25'	8	○	✿	HD	LD	Yellow	Deciduous

This native of the desert Southwest is beloved for its vivid green bark and bright yellow spring flowers. Adapted to super-dry conditions, paloverde grows fast and rank in the depths of high summer heat in the desert under irrigation. Paloverde self-sows readily where there's moisture, so one tree can generate a whole neighborhood of them. That's why the introduction of nearly thornless 'Desert Museum', a sterile clone, proved so popular. It provides the same feel as the species without its major

drawbacks. These trees do not adapt to coastal conditions where they're prone to mildew. Inland they thrive in dry heat, porous lean soils, and seasonal water. The species remains a great choice for rural desert homes where conditions are more challenging than in town.

ROBINIA × AMBIGUA 'IDAHOENSIS' (IDAHO LOCUST)

Height	Width	Zone	Sun	Bloom Season	Region			Flower Color	Type
50'	30'	2	O	✿	HD	M	IV	Rose pink	Deciduous

This Idaho locust is among the most tradition-ally beautiful hardy flowering trees for the arid West that's tough enough to take mountain cold. Wisteria-like clusters of rose-pink blooms are generously produced in late spring followed by pods that hold until winter. It is considered a well-behaved alternative to invasive black locust, but be aware of where you plant Idaho locust because its roots are effective water seek-ers. This tree reaches 50 feet at maturity, so it's capable of making big shade for larger home-sites. With no known pests or diseases, Idaho locust is an important shade tree because it's so traditional-looking and widely adaptable.

VITEX AGNUS-CASTUS (CHASTE TREE)

Height	Width	Zone	Sun	Bloom Season	Region			Flower Color	Type
10'	8'	6	◯	✤	LD	C	IV	Blue	Decidu-ous

This is a rare blue-flowered tree that is super drought resistant. Beware that it likes hot climates and may be potentially invasive in a few counties. It's a very ancient tree of Asia Minor where its aromatic foliage has been used as a medicinal plant for millennia. Chaste tree is common in Texas and throughout the South, but it deserves more attention farther west because this is a valuable bee nectar plant that draws a wide range of local species as well as honeybees. Smaller in size, it may prove more shrubby where winters are on the colder side of its tolerance range.

Flowering Tree Selection Matrix

BOTANICAL NAME	COMMON NAME	ZONE	FLOWER COLOR
Acacia baileyana 'Purpurea'	Bailey's Acacia	7	Yellow
Albizia julibrissin	Mimosa	6	Pink
Arbutus unedo	Strawberry Tree	8	White
Bauhinia × blakeana	Hong Kong Orchid Tree	9	Pink
*Chilopsis linearis**	Desert Willow	7	Pink
Chitalpa × tashkentensis	Chitalpa	6	Pale pink
Chorisia speciosa	Silk Floss Tree	9	Magenta
Jacaranda acutifolia	Jacaranda	9	Purple
Lagerstroemia indica hybrids	Crape Myrtle	7	Pinks, white, red, lavender
*Parkinsonia florida**	Blue Paloverde	8	Yellow
Robinia × ambigua 'Idahoensis'	Idaho Locust	2	Rose pink
Vitex agnus-castus	Chaste Tree	6	Blue

*Indicates California native species.

10   Dry and Edible

When a long-lived food plant can be integrated into the ornamental landscape around your home, there's no need for new irrigation or spaces to grow them. What's key is viewing a food plant as designers do by assessing its type, visual interest, and whether it can solve problems in the landscape. For example, a fig tree yields crops every year, sometimes two, while it provides shade over a large area with no more irrigation than most drought-resistant shrubs. Therefore our edible plants here are grouped as we would landscape plants, by type, to aid in the process of design with useful species within the ornamental landscape.

When preparing this list, flowers and color were not the primary criteria. Instead these are selected for their usability and drought resistance.

Trees

Key

Sun			Bloom Season				Region				
●	◑	○	✿	☀	🍁	❄	HD	LD	M	C	IV
SHADE	PARTLY SUNNY	SUN	SPRING	SUMMER	FALL	WINTER	HIGH DESERT	LOW DESERT	MOUN-TAINS	COAST	INLAND VALLEY

FICUS CARICA (FIG)

Height	Width	Zone	Sun	Bloom Season	Region	Flower Color	Type
10'–30'	10'–20'	8	○	✿	LD	Cream	Deciduous

Figs are a very ancient fruit that dates back to biblical times. Figs are divided into those that set fruit once a year and those which also feature a "breba" or first crop in midsummer, then the second crop in late summer or fall. Grow fig trees in a well-drained full sun location where they reach 20 to 30 feet at maturity. These trees prefer dry, warm climates and may suffer diseases where it's too wet or rainy in spring and fall. Dwarf varieties such as 'Petite Negri' grow well in containers more easily brought inside at season's end where fall is too cool to ripen fruit.

Fig Varieties for Residential Gardens

- 'White Adriatic'—Good fresh picked, but especially good for drying. Yellow skin and amber flesh. No breba crop. Ripens late September.
- 'Black Mission'—The most dependable variety for the home orchard. Purple-black skin with red flesh. The breba crop matures in late June, and the second crop matures in August.
- 'Brown Turkey'—Excellent-quality large fruit with a small breba crop every year and a second crop in August. Purple-green skin. Red flesh.
- 'Black Italian'—Everbearing in frost-free climates. A 'Brown Turkey' type, small size suitable for winter protection.

- 'Kadota'—Requires high temperatures and a long growing season to perform well. Yellow-green fruit with amber flesh. Produces both breba and a second crop.
- 'Osborn Prolific'—Performs well only in cool coastal areas. Produces breba and second crops, purple-bronze fruit with amber flesh.
- 'White Genoa'—Good for coastal locations. Large yellow-green fruit with thin skin and strawberry flesh. Ripens when others won't.

LAURUS NOBILIS (SWEET BAY)

Height	Width	Zone	Sun		Bloom Season	Region			Flower Color	Type
30'	20'	8	◑	○	✿	M	C	IV	Cream	Evergreen

The leaves of this Mediterranean tree were a symbol of victory in Ancient Greece. Rich in oils, the laurel is the source of "sweet bay leaves" in the seasoning drawer. They don't hold a candle to those fresh picked from your own drought-resistant tree in the yard. These slow growers are evergreen and long-lived though shrubby in youth; they make an ideal hedge for privacy screens. If the trunk is exposed, bark easily sunburns and blisters. This is a very useful plant because fresh-picked bay leaves placed in stored food containers successfully deters pantry weevils.

OLEA EUROPAEA (OLIVE)

Height	Width	Zone	Sun	Bloom Season	Region			Flower Color	Type
20'–30'	20'–30'	8	O	✿	LD	C	IV	Cream, fruit black	Evergreen

Olives are among the most long-lived drought-resistant trees and many very old specimens adapt nicely to transplanting. This provides you with a large tree for shade, but when grown for fruit it should not be positioned where the canopy overhangs paving, as fruit can cause both stains and accidents. Reserve fruiting olives for spaces away from the house to yield every year for centuries to come.

PUNICA GRANATUM (POMEGRANATE)

Height	Width	Zone	Sun	Bloom Season	Region			Flower Color	Type
8'–15'	20'	8	O	✿	LD	C	IV	Coral red	Deciduous

Pomegranate trees have been cultivated for millennia in dry climates around the world as well as in California and Arizona. In residential gardens this deciduous tree can grow far beyond the deserts, but without summer heat fruit doesn't ripen as sweet. Where late summer heat is absent, such as in the Pacific Northwest, plants are grown in containers and brought indoors for ripening. Pomegranate trees are self-fruitful and average 8 to 15 feet tall, commonly with multiple trunks. 'Wonderful' is the most common market pomegranate, but many other varieties are available with unique flavors, different colors, and smaller stature. Smaller varieties are easily protected from cold with covers to allow them to grow beyond the Zone 8 hardiness rating.

Top Varieties of Pomegranates for Drought-Resistant Gardens

'Wonderful'—The most commonly grown commercial variety.

'Ambrosia'—Identical to 'Wonderful' except fruit is three times larger.

'Sweet'—Preferred for cooler summer climates and container culture.

'Eversweet'—Seedless. Ripens early. Ideal for short growing seasons.

'Pink Satin'—Seedless or seeds very soft. Super sweet.

'Red Silk'—Dwarf to just 6 feet tall. Ideal for containers.

'Kashmir Blend'—Complex flavor often grown for its healthy juice.

Shrubs, Perennials & Vines

CYNARA SCOLYMUS (GLOBE ARTICHOKE)

Height	Width	Zone	Sun	Bloom Season		Region			Flower Color	Type
3'–5'	4'–7'	8	O	✿	☀	LD	C	IV	Purple	Perennial

Along the California coastal foothills you'll find areas where the artichoke has naturalized, proving it is perfectly adapted to the local climate. It's the immature bud of these flowers we eat, but the blooms themselves are highly ornamental, as is the grayish frilly foliage. This plant was a popular art nouveau motif and natural drought resistance ensured those planted would survive the inevitable dry times. Though it's a useful perennial in the kitchen, don't underestimate its ornamental value in the arid garden either.

VITIS VINIFERA (SEEDLESS GRAPES)

Height	Width	Zone	Sun	Bloom Season	Region				Flower Color	Type
Varies	Varies	4	◯	✿	HD	LD	C	IV	Cream	Deciduous

The most famous table grape, 'Thompson Seedless', was discovered in the
Sacramento Valley where it is well adapted to the long, rainless dry season. This,
'Flame Seedless', and other new hybrids are among the best choices for home
gardens. To increase shade, grow grapes on a large beam arbor that ensures all
branches are exposed to plenty of direct sunlight. Grapevines are the most famous
shade-giving arbor-grown food plants and withstand very hot climates. Or grow
grapes on a freestanding wire arbor to increase access and pruning methods that
yield greater harvests. Grapes are vulnerable to mildew when air circulation is
limited or when shaded by nearby trees. A new Pierce's disease spread by the
glassy-winged sharpshooter bug is causing serious problems. All grapes should
be grown on a drip system to prevent moisture stimulation of mildew by damp
surface soils shaded by the foliage.

Unusual Edibles

CARISSA MACROCARPA 'TOMLINSON' (NATAL PLUM)

Height	Width	Zone	Sun	Bloom Season		Region		Flower Color	Type
2'	20'–35'	10	O	✿	☼	LD	C	White, fruit red	Spreading shrub

This dark evergreen tropical shrub with its small gardenia-scented flowers is a native of dry South Africa and has long been a staple for frost-free beach and desert areas of Southern California. This very drought-tolerant shrub is amazingly adapted to sandy soils and accumulated salts in locations where low fertility and high pH are hostile to most other plants. This makes it an exceptional problem solver. The quarter-sized rounded leaves are thick and leathery, which adds great resistance to wind desiccation and sand pitting. Plants produce attractive bright-red edible fruit that follows each flower. Traditionally grown as an ornamental, *Carissa* deserves a fresh look today as a fruiting plant that stands up to drought far better than its tree fruit namesake.

CEREUS REPANDUS A.K.A. CEREUS PERUVIANUS (APPLE CACTUS)

Height	Width	Zone	Sun	Bloom Season		Region		Flower Color	Type
10'	Varies	9	O	✿	☀	LD	C	White, fruit red	Cactus

This large tree-sized branching cactus has few thorns and typically grows as an ornamental in Southern California, where they reach enormous proportions around Los Angeles. It produces smooth-skinned fruits with flesh nearly identical to dragon fruit for slightly colder areas. Decades ago the Israelis brought this cactus to the Middle Eastern desert and began experimenting with it as an orchard crop. With great success they have bred and selected plants to find the most optimal producer for dry

gardens. There is evidence that these cacti can grow in slightly colder areas with minimal frost damage, particularly if protected during the winter.

TIP: A popular way to protect the tender dividing cells at the growing tip of each stem from frost is to cap each with a Styrofoam cup on frosty nights.

HYLOCEREUS UNDATUS (PITAYA DRAGON FRUIT)

Height	Width	Zone	Sun		Bloom Season		Region		Flower Color	Type
Varies	Varies	10	◑	○	✿	☀	LD	C	White, fruit red	Cactus vine

This vine cactus has long been grown in frost-free coastal conditions, so its range is quite limited. However, its incredibly huge white night-blooming flowers are so highly ornamental they were first grown in home gardens strictly as an ornamental. When pollinated, these flowers yield to large white-fleshed fruit that is amazingly sweet. Sometimes it's grown in tandem with other vines on arbors to add visual diversity. Like all cacti it is drought resistant and may grow quickly in sheltered yards and gardens.

OPUNTIA SPP. (PRICKLY PEAR)

Height	Width	Zone	Sun	Bloom Season		Region				Flower Color	Type
Varies	Varies	8	O	✿	☀	HD	LD	C	IV	Many	Cactus

Prickly pear cactus fruit has long been harvested in Mexico and is an important part of the diet of rural villagers in very dry regions. A spine-free version was first grown at the California missions and today those same plants are still growing in local gardens, blooming like crazy every spring. These most drought resistant of all garden plants should be selected for their large fruits that have minimal spines so they are easier to prepare. Seek plants to buy while they are in fruit to ensure you get highly productive individuals.

TIP: Grasp a fruit in metal tongs and hold it over a flame to burn away the spines and glochids before peeling.

ROSA RUGOSA (JAPANESE ROSE)

Height	Width	Zone	Sun	Bloom Season		Region			Flower Color	Type
4'–6'	4'–6'	2	O	⚘	☀	HD	M	IV	Pink, fruit red	Deciduous

In the mountains you'll find the bright red fruits of the Japanese rose standing out bold and beautiful under the early snow. The fruit follows large pink flowers that mature once pollinated into the largest of all rose fruits. Known as rose hips, these fruits are valued for their very high vitamin content. These may be harvested in the fall and dried or frozen for winter use. This curious rose spreads by underground roots that are able to work their way through thin, rocky soils of higher elevations. Over time they become a colony of fruit-bearing upright stems easily propagated through root division. These roses are grown along the coastlines everywhere because they demand little water and stand up to persistent wind and salt air. Hardy to the lowest temperatures, they thrive in the mountains without special care or protection from winter cold.

Edible Landscape Plant Selection Matrix

BOTANICAL NAME	COMMON NAME	ZONE	EDIBLE PART	TYPE
Carissa macrocarpa 'Tomlinson'	Natal Plum	10	Fruit	Shrub
Cereus repandus a.k.a. *Cereus peruvianus*	Apple Cactus	9	Fruit	Cactus
Cynara cardunculus	Cardoon	6	Vegetable	Perennial
Cynara scolymus	Globe Artichoke	8	Vegetable	Perennial
Ficus carica	Fig	8	Fruit	Tree
Foeniculum vulgare	Fennel	4	Herb	Perennial
Hylocereus undatus	Pitaya Dragon Fruit	10	Fruit	Cactus
Laurus nobilis	Sweet Bay	8	Seasoning	Tree
Olea europaea	Olive	8	Fruit	Tree
Opuntia spp.	Prickly Pear	8	Fruit	Cactus
Punica granatum	Pomegranate	8	Fruit	Tree
Rosa rugosa	Japanese Rose	2	Fruit	Shrub
Vitis vinifera	Seedless Grapes	4	Fruit	Vine

Acknowledgments

An author is only as good as the team that supports her. I want to thank all of those who helped me, from the early work with my literary agent, Jeanne Fredericks, and editor, Hannah Elnan, to define what people really want in sustainable gardens. Combined with the editors Bridget Sweet, Kristin Vorce Duran, Emma Reh, and Em Gale, who make my words far better than written—this book is indeed a group effort. I feel deep gratitude for all their efforts to bring flowers back into the fore of American gardens.

Resources

Plant Sellers and Databases

High Country Gardens;
HighCountryGardens.com; 800-925-9387

> *Western natives, hardy dryland
> perennials, mountain succulents,
> and bulbs.*

Las Pilitas Nursery; LasPilitas.com;
805-438-5992

> *California native plants sold
> on-site and online.*

Mountain States Wholesale Nursery;
MSWN.com; 623-247-8509

> *Outstanding database of
> drought-resistant plants.*

Top Wildflower Sources Online and by Catalog

American Meadows; AmericanMeadows
.com; 877-309-7333

Applewood Seed Co.; ApplewoodSeed
.com; 303-431-7333

Western Native Seed; WesternNativeSeed
.com; 719-942-3935

Wildseed Farms; Shop.WildseedFarms
.com; 800-848-0078

Gardens and Parks by Location
CALIFORNIA

Balboa Park; BalboaPark.org; Visitors
Center, 1549 El Prado, Balboa Park, San
Diego, CA 92101; 619-239-0512

> *Historic location for introduction
> of many drought-resistant species
> growing in the park.*

Huntington Botanical Garden; Huntington
.org/Gardens; 1151 Oxford Rd., San
Marino, CA 91108; 626-405-2100

> *Famous estate contains the Desert
> Garden, among the best in the world.*

The Living Desert; LivingDesert.org;
47900 Portola Ave., Palm Desert, CA
92260; 760-346-5694

> *Zoological garden featuring inter-
> national desert plants and wildlife.*

Moorten Botanical Garden;
MoortenBotanicalGarden.com; 1701
S. Palm Canyon Dr., Palm Springs, CA
92264; 760-327-6555

> *Old garden filled with desert plants
> from around the world.*

Rancho Santa Ana Botanic Garden;
RSABG.org; 1500 N. College Ave.,
Claremont, CA 91711

> *Native plants and environmental
> conservation.*

Ruth Bancroft Garden;
RuthBancroftGarden.org; 1552 Bancroft
Rd., Walnut Creek, CA 94598; 925-944-
9352

> *Water-conservative plants for the
> San Francisco Bay Area.*

San Diego Botanic Garden (formerly
known as Quail Botanical Garden);
SDBGarden.org; 230 Quail Gardens Dr.,
Encinitas, CA 92023; 760-436-3036

> *Native and exotic drought-resistant
> plants and succulents.*

San Francisco Botanical Garden; SFBotanicalGarden.org; 1199 9th Ave., San Francisco, CA 94122; 415-368-5406

> *Large collection of drought-resistant species for coastal climates.*

Theodore Payne Foundation for Wild Flowers and Native Plants; TheodorePayne.org; 10459 Tuxford St., Sun Valley, CA 91352; 818-768-1802

> *Best resource for native annuals and perennials and much more.*

UC Davis Arboretum; Arboretum.UCDavis.edu; 1 Shields Ave., Davis, CA 95616; 530-752-4880

> *Exceptional resource for inland Northern California.*

University of California Botanical Garden at Berkeley; BotanicalGarden.Berkeley.edu; 200 Centennial Dr., Berkeley, CA 94720; 510-643-2755

> *Exceptional resource for coastal Northern California.*

SOUTHWEST

Desert Botanical Garden; DBG.org; 1201 N. Galvin Pwy., Phoenix, AZ 85008; 480-941-1225

> *World-famous cacti and succulents plus global desert plant collection.*

Lady Bird Johnson Wildflower Center; Wildflower.org; 4801 La Crosse Ave., Austin, TX 78739; 512-232-0100

> *Dedicated to plants of Texas and wildflowers everywhere.*

Organizations

Arizona Native Plant Society; AZNPS.com

> *Best resource on local native plant species suited to Arizona.*

California Native Plant Society (CNPS); CNPS.org

> *Where to find the local chapter of this society to get specific information and take advantage of plant sales.*

Native Plant Society of Texas; NPSOT.org

> *Best resource on local native plant species suited to Texas.*

UC Master Gardener Program; MG.UCANR.edu

> *Where to find your nearest Master Gardener for help with your project.*

Index

Photo by James Gilmer

About the Author

MAUREEN GILMER is a syndicated garden columnist and author of eighteen books on gardening and landscaping design. She lives in Palm Springs, California, in the heart of the desert.

Find out more at MoPlants.com.